# THE PRELIMINARY PRACTICES OF TIBETAN BUDDHISM

# THE PRELIMINARY PRACTICES OF TIBETAN BUDDHISM

by Geshe Rabten

Translated
by Gonsar Tulku

Compiled
by Georges Driessens

LIBRARY OF TIBETAN WORKS & ARCHIVES

ISBN: 81-85102-62-7

Published by the Library of Tibetan Works & Archives,
Dharamsala, H.P. and printed at Indraprastha Press (CBT),
New Delhi-110002.

# Contents

# Publishers Note

We are happy to bring out this revised edition of the oral teachings of Geshe Rabten, a meditation master and scholar from the Sera Monastic University, Lhasa, Tibet, on the preliminary practices of Tibetan Buddhism.

Besides their authentic Tibetan Buddhist flavour, these oral teachings on the preliminary practices serve as an excellent introduction to the essential philosophy of Tibetan Buddhism now gaining strong scientific and scholarly interest and attention in many countries of the world.

We are sure that the readers will benefit from this revised edition of the teachings of Geshe Rabten.

Gyatso Tsering
Director
September, 1994

# Introduction

To practise dharma, you must first accomplish the five preliminaries, and if this is done properly, all further practices
will develop better. The preliminaries are beneficial not only
in terms of the dharma but also in our daily lives.

Most people want to be given the main practices immediately but do not realize that the person who is unprepared
for them will not achieve the results he expects and will soon
become discouraged. It is for this reason that such practices
cannot be given at the outset. Before constructing a house,
you must level the ground and lay a solid foundation. To
build the house of dharma, you must prepare the mind by
means of the preliminaries. Intellectual understanding is not
enough and must be followed by intensive practice if true
realization is to be gained. A museum approach to the
dharma, merely looking at and recognizing objects, is of no
help whatsoever for inner development. The way to effect
change is to observe the dharma, watching and correcting
the actions of body, speech and mind at all times.

There are various ways of dividing the preliminaries. For
example, in the Gelug tradition there are six preliminaries[1].
But all are concerned with the five basic points. These points
will be explained in the following pages.

Geshe Rabten.

# The Preliminary Practices of Tibetan Buddhism

*"I bow at the Lotus feet of all the Buddhas"*

There are two divisions of the preliminary practices of Tibetan Buddhism:

1. The Ordinary Preliminaries.
2. The Extraordinary Preliminaries.

# I. The Ordinary Preliminaries

These preliminaries consist of four contemplations.

    A. The difficulty of obtaining a perfect human rebirth.
    B. Impermanence and death.
    C. The law of karma.
    D. The misery of samsara.

## A. The Difficulty of Obtaining a Perfect Human Rebirth has Three Aspects

    1. Recognition of the perfect human rebirth.
    2. Contemplation on its value.
    3. Contemplation on its scarcity.

### 1. RECOGNITION OF THE PERFECT HUMAN REBIRTH

A man who finds a nugget of gold must first be aware that it is pure gold, only then will he recognize its great value. Subsequently it will become clear to him that he is unlikely ever to find another, and so he will realize the importance of making good use of it.

This piece of gold is like the perfect human rebirth. We may think that all human beings are the same. However, this is not so, since many differences exist and not all humans have obtained the perfect rebirth. Such a rebirth is unique, and must possess eighteen specific qualities. It is therefore called in Tibetan "dal jor gyi mi lus". "dal" means leisure or rest, and implies that there is freedom to practise the dharma. "jor" means endowments.

# 4 The Preliminary Practices of Tibetan Buddhism

## a. THE EIGHT FREEDOMS

1. Not to be born as a hell sentient being. In this realm there is continual and unbearable suffering. Not a word of the dharma is ever heard. A man whose arm is on fire cannot think of meditation for even a second. Killing and other similar deeds are the main causes for rebirth in this realm.

2. Not to be born a hungry ghost. The beings in this realm can never satisfy their hunger and thirst and have no opportunity to practise the dharma. If you were forced to go without food for even one day, you would find it very difficult to do anything. However, this is nothing compared to the miseries of the hungry ghosts. The main causes for rebirth in this realm are greed, avarice, and covetousness.

3. Not to be born as an animal. The misery of this realm is quite obvious. The ignorance and extreme stupidity of animals prevent them from ever coming close to the dharma.

   If all the religious teachers of the world were together and preached to a dog, instead of listening he would wag his tail in the hope of food. The main causes for rebirth in this realm are sexual misconduct, calling others by animal names as a form of abuse, and reluctance to learn the dharma.

4. Not to be born as a deva. Devas of the form and formless worlds enjoy the bliss of samadhi for a very long period of time, whereas devas in the realm of desire are totally involved in sensual pleasures. The happiness they experience accounts for the lack of motivation amongst most devas to practise the dharma. Life in these spheres is like the enjoyment gained from living off a large sum of borrowed money. When the funds run out difficulties arise. The main causes for rebirth in this realm are practising skilful deeds without the motivation to attain en-

lightenment, or specifically wishing to be reborn as a deva.

5. Not to be born in a place of no dharma. From the point of view of the dharma, the life of a human being who works, eats, sleeps and wakes to work again for only the temporal gratifications of this life is no different from that of an animal.

6. To be free from perverted views. Although a person may be born in a country where the dharma flourishes and may be surrounded by many teachers, if he has erroneous beliefs he will not be able to benefit from these favorable conditions. Perverted views are dangerous because they destroy the seeds of merit accumulated in former lives and close the door to further development.

7. To be free from deluded practices. Some people spend their energy on wrong practices. For instance, animal sacrifice, asceticism, and giving the name of the dharma to paths which in fact produce opposite results. The story of Angulimala is a good example of such practices; his teacher taught him that the only way he could attain freedom was by killing a thousand people and wearing a rosary made of their fingers. While searching for his last victim, he met the Buddha who preached to him and showed him the path by means of which he finally attained arhatship.

8. To be free from stupidity. No matter how much a man who has no intelligence is taught, he will never retain the smallest glimpse of knowledge.

Repeated contemplation on your own lives would not fail to reveal that if death came at this moment, the non-virtuous actions you have committed since the beginning of your life would constitute sufficient cause for immediate rebirth in one of the three lower realms. Contemplation on the causes for rebirth in these worlds should help to eliminate any remaining doubts concerning this certainty. However, all human beings have the potential to possess the eight freedoms.

You are alive and free from the obstacles of wrong views and stupidity, and by discrimination between right and wrong you are able to practise skilful deeds.

You should rejoice at this great opportunity presented by the precious rebirth and use it in the right way before it is lost once again. A criminal who has escaped from a mob feels great joy at regaining his freedom, but at the same time fears his recapture. Also, a blind man who has caught a flea that was bothering him, would be a fool to let it go again. In the same way, you will feel compelled by this realization not to waste a single moment of your precious rebirth. This is turn will establish in your minds the strong motivation necessary for the practice of higher meditations.

b. THE TEN ENDOWMENTS

*(1) Five personal endowments*

1. To be born a human being.
2. To be born in a central country. (This means wherever the dharma is flourishing.)
3. To be endowed with complete faculties. This means to have a body without defects and not deficient in any of the five senses.
4.. To respect and have faith in the Buddha and not to have committed any of the five heinous crimes,[2] namely, killing one's father or mother, killing an arhat, shedding the blood of a Buddha or causing a schism in the Sangha or between a Buddha and the Sangha.
5. To have faith in the Tripitaka[3] and the desire to practise its teaching. Initially, for most people it is difficult to have faith in the Buddha and the Dharma, since such faith is the result of gradual spiritual development and growth.

*(2) Five circumstantial endowments*

6. To be born in a time when the Buddha has appeared. There are many dark aeons without Buddhas and only very few illuminated by their presence.

7. To be born in a time when the Buddha has taught. In some circumstances Buddhas appear and pass away without teaching.

8. To be born when the teaching of the Buddha is alive is to enjoy particular good fortune. At present there still are teachers propounding the dharma.

9. To be born where the dharma is practised. The example of others who are practising is a great encouragement.

10. To be born in a place where you find a means of support. Material necessities become available when all your energies are dedicated to the practice of dharma: Luipa was living on the offal of a fish and Milarepa lived on nettle soup. How can you do this while you are so attached to pleasure?

It is very rare to be endowed with these eighteen conditions at one time. When you recognize the true value of your precious rebirth you are like the man who realizes that he has found gold. Brass, copper and other metals shine like gold, but gold has its own inimitable qualities.

At this moment you are midway between the higher and lower realms. If you fail to act virtuously, you will definitely lose this precious opportunity. To be convinced of this point brings about the decision to practise dharma.

## 2. CONTEMPLATION ON THE GREAT VALUE OF A PERFECT HUMAN REBIRTH

By means of this rebirth, through work and study, you can attain all worldly goals and happinesses. However, these are not important compared with the goal of the full enlightenment of Buddhahood. Liberation is achieved by the correct use of the precious rebirth and is not automatically produced by the eighteen conditions. Even if you possessed all the wealth of the universe, it would not help to attain liberation.

Until now you have been unable to raise your head above

the misery of samsara. By abandoning the unskilful karma and by practising bodhichitta, great compassion, great loving kindness and the various levels on the path, you can, not only attain liberation, but also supreme enlightenment in this very life. At this stage you will realize that you have the ability to practise the dharma.

### 3. CONTEMPLATION ON THE SCARCITY OF THE PERFECT HUMAN REBIRTH

The purpose of this teaching is not that it should be read through and kept in a book, but that it should be used for contemplation. Only if you do this at least three times a day can you hope to effect a definite change in your mind. You are quite willing to dedicate your energies to a highly paid job; likewise the follower of dharma must be willing to exert all his energy in the practice. If these contemplations are not done properly they will not yield fruit, and eventually doubts will arise as to their effectiveness and validity.

You may think that so far your life has been wasted, and form the intention to do better in your next rebirth. This is a false hope. You must realize the unlikelihood of ever finding such favorable conditions again. Contemplation on the scarcity of the human rebirth will help to avoid the forming of such a hope.

This contemplation is done in the order: (a) by number, (b) by example and (c) by cause.

#### a. BY NUMBER

From the hells to the deva worlds, the number of beings decreases in each realm. The population of hells far outnumbers that of the hungry ghosts, realm, and it is obvious that animals are much more numerous than human beings. Even in this human realm very few are endowed with the eighteen conditions. Why is this rebirth so scarce and why are the lower realms so heavily populated? It is because of the immense number of unskilful deeds committed. To act skilfully you need a sound understanding of the law of karma, and this is as difficult to acquire as for a stream to run uphill.

In the *Bodhisattvacaryavatara* the Bodhisattva Shantideva said:

> How rare is this precious life!
> If a man who is endowed with it fails to benefit
>     from it,
> How difficult it will be for him to acquire it again!

And,

> With the boat of this precious life
> You can cross the waters of samsara.
> How rare to find this boat!
> O ignorant one, do not fall asleep now!

Milarepa, addressing the hunter, said:

> I have been told that it is rare to acquire a precious human life.
> If your life is such, then I can find no truth in these
>     words.

Only the shape differentiates the hunter from the animal he hunts, for both are dominated by delusions.

Those endowed with the eighteen conditions are very few because unskilful deeds are numerous and virtues are rare. You may learn this not only by number but also by example.

## b. BY EXAMPLE

The Bodhisattva Shantideva quoting the sutras in the *Bodhisattvacaryavatara*, illustrates this point very accurately by an example which should not merely be taken as a tale but should be used for intensive contemplation.

At the bottom of a vast ocean of unfathomable depth lives a blind turtle that surfaces once every hundred years. It remains on the surface for only one instant and then sinks back down to the ocean bed. On the surface floats a golden yoke constantly in motion, driven hither and thither by the winds and tides. The turtle symbolizes any sentient being, the surface of the ocean, the fortunate realms. The turtle is blind as is our wisdom-eye which, veiled by ignorance, cannot discern right from wrong. Just as the turtle is encumbered by its shell, so obstacles created by our body, speech and mind hinder us when we seriously try to practise dharma, rather than just to read books and recite prayers. The turtle lives at the bottom of the ocean symbolizing that we usually dwell in the lower realms. It surfaces for only a second and then sinks again, and it seems almost impossible that it should ever succeed in passing its head through the floating yoke. Similarly it is even more difficult to obtain this short human life and to have the will to practise the dharma.

Long periods of time pass without the presence of a Buddha, and when Buddhas appear, they very rarely give teachings. If we are born in an illumined aeon, to meet with a living dharma tradition is to be especially fortunate, for it is not the numerous scriptures that matter but their correct use.

By contemplating their causes we will see more clearly how unique it is to be endowed with the eighteen conditions.

c. BY CAUSE

A farmer who wishes to harvest a crop of wheat must first sow the seed. Similarly, to gain this precious rebirth requires a specific seed: maintaining the purity of moral discipline. Among the different levels of moral commitment we are mainly concerned with the abandonment of the ten non-virtuous deeds:

1. *Three actions of the body:* killing, stealing and sexual misconduct;
2. *Four actions of speech:* lying, slander, abuse and idle talk;
*Three actions of mind:* covetousness, harmful thoughts and wrong views.

Milarepa said:

> Rare indeed are those endowed with a perfect rebirth, for it is hard to meet beings who keep pure morality.

You may think that since the world population is increasing your chances of obtaining a human life again are becoming greater. However, it is the perfect rebirth that is important. The purity of the ten virtues as a basic seed and, in addition, the practices of giving, patience, and the other perfections free from the eight worldly concerns[4] as circumstantial agents, form the link for a perfect rebirth in the future. The question you must ask is whether or not you have its cause within yourselves. In a shop there are numerous articles for sale, but before buying you must first check your purse to see if you can purchase any of them.

Morality (shila) is the foundation of all attainments especially of shamatha and dhyana[5]. From the first realization of dharma until the attainment of Buddhahood you must progress through the threefold training (trisiksha) of shila, samadhi and prajna. This is illustrated by the Wheel of Dharma. The following explanation is one interpretation of its symbolism.

The hub of the wheel represents shila-shiksha; it is the central part because all attainments depend on it. The rim is samadhi, for it keeps the mind collected. The eight spokes are the sharp weapons of prajna which sever ignorance. On both sides of the wheel are two deer facing each other and looking upwards in the same direction, signifying means (upaya) and wisdom (prajna), both of which are inseparable from the attainment of buddhahood.

## B. Contemplation on Impermanence and Death has Three Parts

1. Contemplation on the certainty of death.
2. Contemplation on the uncertainty of the time of death.
3. The realization that at the time of death the dharma is the only saviour.

### I. CONTEMPLATION ON THE CERTAINTY OF DEATH

As long as we are samsaric beings in any of the three worlds, there is no freedom from death.

> Nor in the sky, nor in the midst of the sea, nor yet
> in the clefts of the mountains, nowhere in the
> world is there any place where having entered one
> will not be overcome by death.

It is impossible to find a body that is not subject to death; even the great Indian pandits like Nagarjuna and mahasiddhas endowed with realization and powers had to leave the body. Buddha Shakyamuni himself also passed away, demonstrating to all sentient beings the impermanence of all conditioned phenomena[6].

In short, when death comes the skill and knowledge of all the doctors of this world are of no avail. Therefore you will realize that the dharma is your only means of escaping death.

Guru Phadampa Sangay said:

> O people of Dhingri, at the very moment that follows birth, you are already in the grip of death. Hurry then, there is no time to lose!

You are like the sheep taken to the slaughter house. Every minute brings death closer. Your black karma causes you to fear death in the same way as the criminal on his way to the execution block.

Milarepa said:

> Impermanence is like the spreading shadow of a mountain at sunset. No matter how hard you run from it, the darkness will finally overtake you. Therefore I find no escape.

As a result of previous karma, you have obtained this human life. It is not within your power to add even a minute to its span. Milarepa said that our body is like an old house with a leaking roof which gradually deteriorates under the rains of years and months, and the drops of days and hours. Although this body is not a strong edifice, you must use it for the achievement of enlightenment.

Some may not find these teachings very pleasant, but to limit explanations to subjects which are agreeable does not lead to the real meaning of the dharma. As a reminder of the omnipresence of death, siddhas and tantric deities are depicted with ornaments of bones, with skull cups, and so forth. When this point is clearly realized, you will decide to start the practice soon.

## 2. CONTEMPLATION ON THE UNCERTAINTY OF TIME OF DEATH

These aspects of death are clearly evident but until now this knowledge has not acted as an impetus for the practice of dharma. When you understand the uncertainty of the time of death, you will develop the necessary inner motivation to begin practising at once. If it was possible to forecast the time of death, you could establish a program for your life. But this is not so. Even age is not a guarantee. Generally the old die before the young, but this does not necessarily hold true when you consider individual cases. Neither wealth, power, wisdom, youth nor rank make any difference, nor does sickness or good health, for even a healthy person may die at any moment. Who can point out the one amongst you who will die first?

Within you are many causes for death and only a few means for protecting life. Four hundred and twenty four potential illnesses are spread throughout the body like an oil stain on paper and no medicine can cure them permanently. Even after you have eliminated one, the cause for another to arise at any time still remains. Externally, life is threatened by animals, spirits, human beings and the natural elements.

This physical body is made up of the four elements: earth, water, fire and air. When these are in perfect balance you remain healthy, but since they are generally imbalanced you are subject to sickness. These elements are like four snakes in a bamboo rod. If they are to remain calm, their heads must be level, otherwise one will harm the others. Most people die because one element predominates over the others. Since the body is inseparable from the elements you would do well to contemplate them in order to understand this point.

In general these fragile aspects of the body and the action of time attack and shorten your life. Normally you are unaware that time is constantly unwinding the rope of life. If you can become conscious of these facts they can teach and help you.

Life is as unsteady as the flame of a butter lamp in the wind, and even those very things which maintain and facilitate life may turn out to be causes of death. People can die from eating harmful food or become victims of car accidents, and so forth.

Milarepa said:

> When you young people are together,
> You have absolutely no awareness of death,
> Yet it strikes like a thunderbolt.

When you hear news of war, you fear for your life but in fact the danger of death is always present. To witness the sudden death of a healthy person reminds you of life's uncertainty and gives you a momentary glimpse of the possibility of your own death since you are no different.

Gyalsay Thogmed Zangpo said:

> Despite the fact that you cannot be certain of living throughout the night, you make preparations as though for eternal life. This is a sure sign that fear and regret will arise at the time of death.

This is true since your actions are motivated by worldly aims.

Nagarjuna said:

> Life is so tenuous and beset by many dangers; it is more fragile and unsteady than a bubble blown to and fro by the wind. How truly astonishing is someone who believes that after breathing in he will breathe out again or that he will awake from a night's sleep.

> Even if your hair and clothes were on fire, you should not concern yourself with them, since you could use that moment to stop rebirth. Nothing is more important than that.

The great gurus of Tibet used to continue their meditation despite painful wounds. Being mindful of this you should also exert yourself and meditate as much as possible, continuing the practice even into your periods of sleep.

At this moment you will decide to start the practice immediately.

## 3. THE REALIZATION THAT AT THE TIME OF DEATH DHARMA IS THE ONLY HELP

How are you to use the practice at that time? Through contemplation on the experience of death.

Death may be natural as caused by disease, or unnatural as in the case of an accident. The processes in each case are different. The explanation which follows is that of a natural death.

The experience begins when the doctors give up all hope. Normally you are able to savor many different tastes but a dying person cannot even drink water. His lips and tongue, which have been the source of much trouble during his life, can barely utter a single word. To clothe his body with rich garments and ornate jewellery is of no use, for they provide neither warmth nor adornment. They are like ornaments on rocks and wood. No one in this world can help a dying man. He must depart alone leaving everything behind, and cannot take even a single hair with him.

The proper practice of dharma during your life is the only real help. When you realize this, then the decision to practise purely and wholeheartedly will arise. You should be aware that your death will one day come and therefore you should begin to prepare immediately. Through acquaintance with the practice, you will have the strength to face the fears and sorrows that arise at death. If you can keep the mind firmly on the necessary practices at the time of death or if you can remember with strong awareness the form of the Buddha worshipped during your life, then the chances for freedom or for a favorable rebirth are good. However, if you have neglected the dharma you will experience strong regret and distress and will die utterly confused.

When death comes the four elements, which are like your legs supporting the consciousness, lose their power, all physical control is lost and the mind becomes separated from the body. During the process two types of signs occur:

1. Outer signs perceived by those around the dying person.
2. Inner signs which the person himself experiences.

Firstly the power of the earth element fails:

1. Bodily control is lost.

2.  The dying person experiences a heat haze like hot air rising on a road, a sign that the water element will fail next.

Secondly the power of the water element fails:

1.  The body becomes like dry wood. It loses its lustre and color, and the moisture in the mouth and eyes disappears.
2.  The dying person experiences space filled with light smoke, a sign that the fire element will fail next.

Thirdly the power of the fire element fails:

1.  The body becomes cold. If this coldness spreads from the head to the heart an unfortunate rebirth is indicated, whereas if it begins at the feet and spreads upwards to the heart, this denotes a fortunate rebirth.
2.  The dying person experiences sparks of fire in the darkness.

Lastly the power of the air element fails:

1.  Breathing accelerates, and the inhalations become shallower. The exhalations become stronger until finally breathing stops after a long exhalation.
2.  The dying person experiences a dim motionless light.

From that moment until the being enters the *bardo* state fears and illusions disappear, the rough awareness of self is forgotten. A meditator will remain calmly concentrated in his practice throughout the four stages, being aware of his present experience and foreseeing what will follow. Since outer manifestations of life have ceased, people around him may think that the person is already dead and they may wish to dispose of the corpse. But, since the inner experiences may still continue for some days, if the body is then buried or cremated it is the same as killing the person.

During life the left and right nadis (energy channels) are knotted to the central nadi which makes circulation through it impossible. At death the control of the body and the power to keep these knots tight is lost. The central nadi is then freed from obstruction.

From this point onwards there are no further visible signs. Now the person experiences an even light similar to that which spreads across the sky before the moon rises. This happens when the white cell received from the father which during life remains at the crown chakra (psychophysical centre) descends to the heart chakra. Next the dying person experiences a dim red light such as pervades the sky at sunset. This occurs when the red cell, the fertilizing force originating from the mother, ascends from the navel chakra to the heart chakra by way of the central nadi (it rises because it is of the nature of fire).

When these two cells meet at the heart chakra the next experience which has two stages begins. Firstly, there is complete darkness, secondly, the dying person becomes unconscious. The longer this state of profound unconsciousness lasts the more beneficial it is for the next stage, the last and most appropriate for the practice.

The person now experiences empty space devoid of form or color which, however, is not shunyata. Consciousness is now in its subtlest form and will not become more refined. For ordinary people who do not know how to make use of it, this state arises and passes and is wasted. However, a person advanced in tantric practices is able to transform this most subtle state of consciousness into meditation on shunyata. In this way, Tsongkhapa as well as many other siddhas realized enlightenment.

Generally, after this stage the two cells separate and leave the body: the red cell as blood from the nose and the white cell through the urinary canal. During sleep and at death it is beneficial to lie in the lion posture in which these two signs become visible. It was thus lying on his right side that the Buddha left his human form.

The consciousness leaves the heart chakra and immediately enters the *bardo* body. The *bardo* is a very difficult phase in which the being has no freedom but is driven helplessly by the force of his own karma towards a new body, thus once more beginning the cycle of rebirth.

The dharma exhorts you to make use of the experience of death for the attainment of liberation. Therefore, in it you will find your greatest help. The results obtained depend on the capacities of the individual; a very intelligent person can attain buddhahood and a man of medium intelligence will be able to obtain a favorable rebirth in order to continue the practice.

To strengthen the former contemplations you can recite the following prayer:

To all the Buddhas I pray:

> Please grant your blessings to enable me to real-
> ize that this perfect rebirth, acquired only once, is
> quickly destroyed, and is hard to find again. May
> I be able to take the essential meaning of this life
> without being distracted by purposeless actions.

## C. Contemplation on the Law of Karma

Karma means action or deed. There are two main types of karma:

1. Samsaric, which ripens in any of the six realms of existence.
2. Non-samsaric, which is free from the possibility of rip-
   ening in any of the three unfortunate realms.

The karma of ordinary beings is of the first kind and the karma of arya beings[7] is of the second.

### THERE ARE MANY DIVISIONS OF
### SAMSARIC KARMA

a. UNSKILFUL KARMA—which results in suffering.

How is unskilful karma produced? When, for instance, you

feel irritated with someone, a strong attachment to the "I" arises and you feel that the relative self which works, eats, studies and dies, has true independent existence. This is like someone walking in the dark and mistaking a length of rope lying on the ground for a snake. He feels afraid because he fails to realize that it is only a rope. In the same way, you feel irritated because your ignorance obscures the true nature of relative self and you cling to it as if it were self-existent. However, it is not the relative self which is negated, because if it is, then what is it that works, eats and so forth? Unless you can make a clear distinction between the relative self and your conditioned view of it which stems from ignorance, you cannot realize shunyata.

This ignorance is the basis of all afflictions (klesa), because hatred, attachment and the other defilements arise from it depending on varied stimuli. Afflictions give rise, for example, to the desire to harm people. When such a desire arises mental karma is created, and this leaves an impression or seed in the stream of consciousness which comes to fruition when the necessary conditions prevail. Mental karma is created more quickly than that produced by action of the body or speech. In a single minute many kinds of mental karma can be created. If this desire to harm increases to the extent that it is expressed through bodily action or speech, then the imprint left on the stream of consciousness is even deeper.

What happened this morning is past, but because your stream of consciousness continues, you remember it. Countless types of virtuous and non-virtuous karma are stored within the mind. For example, if you lied in your childhood, the seed will remain in you and bear fruit when the right time comes, unless you have already experienced its effect or have eliminated this karma by suitable practices.

b. SKILFUL KARMA—which is the cause of happiness.

The following is an example of the production of skilful

karma. If you see someone who is about to kill a bird, this provokes a feeling of compassion. Subsequently, if the will to save its life arises, skilful mental karma is created, which will leave a positive impression on your stream of consciousness. Then, should this compassionate intention take the form of action through body or speech and the bird is freed, the strength of this skilful karma is increased. The result is happiness for yourself and others.

## TWO ASPECTS OF KARMA

1. Individual karma is created by one person and he alone will experience the results.
2. Collective karma is produced by a group of people and the results are experienced by that same group in similar circumstances. It is because they have collected the same cause that when the circumstances are present people will face analogous sufferings and joys.

At the time of the Buddha, a group of arya bhikshunis were living in a hermitage together with an ordinary woman who worked as their cook. One day all the huts caught fire and the aryas, in order to escape from the flames, flew up into the air by means of their miraculous powers. However, the force of their karma was such that they were pulled down again towards the blaze. At that moment, the most spiritually advanced of the bhikshunis had a glimpse into the past lives of the group. She saw that at one time as children, they had burnt a Pratyekabuddha (individual Buddha) in his hut, and the cook had been the only one to oppose this deed. This having been revealed to them the bhikshunis accepted their karma and perished in the flames, while the cook was able to save her life by escaping through a drain.

Two further aspects of karma concern the intention and the accomplishment of an action.

In the case where both intention and accomplishment are either skilful or unskilful, the result will either be beneficial or non-beneficial. If, however, intention and accomplishment are not in unison, a mixed result will come from the action. For example, if you give alms to a beggar but do so in a disrespectful way, you will collect the causes for future wealth, but there will be difficulties like those arising over an inheritance to which you are lawfully entitled.

The heaviness of a particular karma depends on the following:

1. The object: actions directed towards your father, mother, gurus, bodhisattvas, the sick or the helpless produce a stronger result.
2. The subject: the result of a particular action will be heavier for a person who has taken vows.
3. The motivation: strong hatred or desire affects the power of karma.
4. The manner: the way in which an action is carried out also influences the result.

Karma arises from the three poisons. If you steal out of an attachment to property you are motivated by the affliction of desire. If you kill an animal out of anger, you are motivated by the affliction of hatred. If you kill out of the belief that it is in some way beneficial, you are governed by the affliction of ignorance. This ignorance, however, is not as deep as that which holds the ego as self-existent, the root of all afflictions.

## DIVISION OF KARMA INTO THROWING AND ACCOMPLISHING KARMA

1. Throwing karma: this throws sentient beings into the different realms of existence.
2. Accomplishing karma: this is responsible for the various qualities which differentiate beings and their living conditions.

These can combine in the following ways:

(a) When the throwing and the accomplishing karma are skilful, the result is a good rebirth and happy living conditions. The main causes for rebirth as a human are restraint from killing and the pure observance of morality. If you refrain from stealing and harming people, and practise giving (dana) your life will be endowed with all the necessary material facilities. If you have dignity and independence, this is mainly the result of abandoning pride and practising humility and respect while the practice of patience is the main cause for a sound body.

(b) When throwing and accomplishing karma are unskilful the result is rebirth in the lower realms where mental and physical suffering of all kinds are experienced from birth until death.

(c) If throwing karma is unskilful, but accomplishing karma is skilful, then an unfavorable rebirth will result but the living conditions will be agreeable. For example, if a being is reborn as a pet dog, he has taken rebirth in one of the lower realms. However, the fact that he faces very little suffering, is of a pleasant appearance and has met a kind owner is the result of his skilful accomplishing karma.

(d) An example of skilful throwing karma and unskilful accomplishing karma is a human being whose life is fraught with many difficulties.

## OTHER CHARACTERISTICS OF KARMA

1. An action of body or speech that is unintentional.
2. An intention that is not completed through physical action or speech.
3. The intention and deed are both committed.
4. Powerful karma: the results of which can be clearly perceived in the same life.
5. Karma experienced in the next life.
6. Karma experienced in the third or subsequent lives.

7. The certainty of karma: the results of an action must inevitably be experienced.
8. An action can produce great results. A young woman with pure motivation gave alms to the Buddha. He prophesied when and where she would attain pratyekabuddhahood as a result of that action. Her husband, however, could not accept that so small an action could have such a result. The Buddha in reply explained that as a tall tree grows from a small seed, the result of a seed of karma is immeasurable.
9. If no seed is sown no effect will arise as in the case of the cook who worked for the arya bhikshunis.
10. A seed of karma never dies. Unless it is eliminated by the practice of dharma, such a seed is dormant until the right conditions bring about its germination.

You may wonder whether the Buddha through his infinite compassion can assist in the elimination of the unskilful karma of a certain being. All beings have accumulated innumerable unskilful deeds which will inevitably result in suffering and misery. Out of compassion the Buddha has shown how karma may be destroyed and thereby eliminate suffering. However, it is entirely up to the individual whether or not this is to be achieved.

A doctor may have great sympathy for a patient and give him the best treatment, but it is up to the patient to follow the prescribed cure. Samsara would have ended long ago if the Buddha's mercy alone could liberate all beings. His compassion even surpasses the powerful love of self. It is like the sun shining equally on all things. Yet if a pot is upside down how can the sunlight enter it?

If karma is certain and no relationship has been established with the Buddha in terms of faith and practice, then change is impossible. Even where such a relationship does exist, change is very difficult. The Buddha's influence can be effective in the case of uncertain karma provided a connection has been established. For example, the life span is determined by previous karma but death may occur before its exhaustion because of actions in this life. It is in this sphere that the Buddha's influence may be felt, for by his compassion he can remove the causes for a premature death.

A man's life span is like a butter lamp which may go out either because the butter is finished or because of a gust of wind. The Buddha can only prevent this second occurrence.

Karma is dangerous and, in order to uproot the afflictions which lead to unskilful deeds, you must practise meditation. For a clear understanding of the nature of afflictions, you must know about the primary and especially about the secondary consciousness. The latter is divided into fifty-one mental factors (ciatta), as explained clearly in the *AbhiDharmasamuccaya* of Asanga. Its correct study enables you to ascribe to each action, virtuous or non-virtuous, the mental factors responsible for it. Karma is a very difficult subject to grasp. It is important to know its different aspects and thus to understand that the various conditions among beings and the experiences they undergo are not the result of mere chance. It is easy to see the external effects resulting from a particular cause, but the law of karma and its fruit is extremely complex.

## THERE ARE THREE WAYS TO UNDERSTAND PHENOMENA

1.  Through the direct application of the senses.
2.  By means of logic and analysis as in the case of shunyata.
3.  Reliance on the knowledge of the Buddha.

Karma belongs to this third category. Only the Buddha is able to trace all the causes responsible for a particular phenomenon such as, for example, the reasons for each of the colors in a peacock's feather.

## D. Contemplation on the Misery of Samsara

### 1. THE SIX REALMS

Rebirth in any of the realms of existence is conditioned by karma. Unskilful karma leads to the three unfortunate realms (hells, hungry ghosts and animals) while skilful karma leads to the three fortunate realms (men, asuras and devas).

Of the three lower realms the animal world is very evident to human beings because they have a permanent karmic relationship with it. However, they do not have this contact with the worlds of the hungry ghosts and the hells. But the mere fact that most people cannot see them is not a sufficient reason to deny their existence. To deny that a person is thinking just because his thoughts are not seen is nonsensical. If at present a person cannot establish a connection with these worlds it is because his mind is not yet developed, and his knowledge resembles the dew drop on a blade of grass compared to the ocean of Buddha's wisdom. To reject the existence of these realms on such a basis is like a blind man who stubbornly refuses to admit the existence of color. The understanding of these realms will be improved with the conviction of karma and its resulting fruits.

#### a. HELLS

There are cold and hot hells. Cold hells are the result of stealing, holding wrong views about the dharma, inflicting suffering occasioned by cold on others, and so forth. The various forms of destroying life, among many other causes, lead to rebirth in the hot hells.

When a person is dying certain signs provoked by his karma become manifest and these may indicate his place of rebirth. Some people may feel extremely cold and beg for warmth. This extreme cold gives rise to a desire for warmth and this craving throws the person into the hot hells. This happens because the seeds of karma ripen at death and slowly appear, just as the venom from a snakebite gradually spreads throughout the body. When the experience is reversed, the person's aversion to heat and his craving for cold cause rebirth in the cold hells. By being aware of such things it will become easier to believe in the existence of these realms.

Volcanoes can be a possible example of hot hells, where consciousness enters the lava and molten rock. The bodies of the beings engulfed there become inseparable from the flames, in the same way that in a red hot ember the coal has assumed the nature of fire.

Likewise, the polar regions may serve as a possible example of cold hells. There the bodies of the beings are inseparable from the ice and they experience indescribable suffering.

When a being is reborn in hell three conditions combine together: the cause, the place and the body that experiences the suffering.

In the *Bodhisattvacaryavatara*, the Bodhisattva Shantideva asks:

> Who has created this burning iron floor,
> the guards who inflict the pain and the raging fires,
>     from where do they come?
> The Tathagata says that all these phenomena are
>     the projection of the evil mind.

Although the hells are mental projections and not self-existent places, they are as real as the human world but are not like the dream state—in which no actual suffering is experienced.

Life in the hells is extremely long and varies according to the different causes. Because of very heavy karma, some beings will remain there until the destruction of the world. Where will they be afterwards? There are millions of worlds, and if their karma is not exhausted, those beings will take rebirth in other worlds under similar circumstances, in the same way as a prisoner whose term is not up is transferred to another jail to complete his sentence.

You can meditate on the hells either by choosing one particular hell, contemplating its sufferings, their causes and finally examining whether these causes are present within you or not, or by contemplating your own impermanence, death and rebirth in the hells. If you find it difficult to imagine yourself as a hell being and you think that you have not gathered the causes for rebirth there during this life, you should realize that these may lie in previous existences. Also, by remembering the uncertainty of the time of death, thoughts such as "I am not dead yet" can be countered.

All changes in nature have both causes and conditions. This is a natural law and is easily apprehensible. Knowing the seed you can foresee the fruit. Although the same law applies to changes within the mind, most people refuse to accept it. When a seed bears fruit it gives rise to a new form. When a human being dies a new form originates conditioned by previous actions.

From a very early age a child may instinctively perform unskilful deeds because of his prior acquaintance with such actions in a past life. Why is it so difficult to produce good karma? Skilful deeds are like good handwriting and come as a result of practice. Through intense investigation you can find the proof of your previous existences. Only when you are convinced of rebirth will contemplation on the six realms be effective. Such explanations will never be satisfactory unless you can examine the teachings for yourself by applying the three ways of understanding phenomena.

The Buddha said:

> Judge my teachings with good reasons in the way that a man assays a piece of gold, weighing it, cutting it, melting it until he is certain that it is gold. Do not follow my teachings only out of respect for me.

### b. HUNGRY GHOSTS

Unless you have spiritual attainments you cannot make contact with this realm. Avarice and greed for possessions cause rebirth in this state. Because hungry ghosts were preoccupied with possessions in their former life, this karma continues to cause them to hunger for such things. Even if a mountain of food is placed before them or water with which to quench their thirst, they cannot see them. They remain in this state for thousands of years. Their bodies are emaciated, their stomachs bloated, and they have no strength. In summer, the moonlight burns them and they freeze in the winter sun. If you went without food for a few days, you would rapidly lose strength and would eventually die of starvation. If these hungry ghosts could die like this it would curtail their sufferings, yet they must continue to live thus until their karma is exhausted.

These conditions apply to hungry ghosts in general but some suffer from specific afflictions. There are those who can see food and water but when they try to reach them, obstacles arise in their path which cause them fear and frighten them away. Others, when they drink the water they have thirsted for, find that it turns to pus or poison or other substances which cause them unbearable suffering. In this world there are various spirits with powers to help or harm humans. Some enjoy a few pleasures and possessions but because of their intense greed they act as though they have nothing. Such spirits are always full of harmful thoughts and are constantly urged by their throwing karma to commit further unskilful deeds which only lead them to lower rebirths.

However, these beings will not always remain as hungry ghosts, nor yourselves as humans. They experience this realm as a result of their deeds, and if your thoughts and actions produce the cause for such rebirth then you too will be obliged to experience it. Therefore you must examine your greed to determine whether you hold the seed for future existence as a hungry ghost. Each person will take rebirth according to his deserts.

c. ANIMALS

The suffering of animals is easily apprehended. They are weak, powerless and endanger their lives for the smallest unskilful action. Human beings add greatly to their suffering, beating, butchering and eating them. They endure heat, cold and hunger but their greatest misery results from their stupidity and complete lack of wisdom. Once a being falls into this realm due to acquaintance with unskilful actions, it is very difficult for him to attain human rebirth again. Animals lack everything they should have and are endowed with everything of which they should be free.

Rebirth in this realm is mainly caused by sexual misconduct:

1.  Pertaining to object: it is considered improper to perform the sexual act with one's father or mother, with a bhikshu or a bhikshuni or with the partner of another person.
2.  Pertaining to time: it is improper to have sexual intercourse on full moon or new moon days or on any special day of religious observance; with a woman during menstrual time, pregnancy, or while nursing a baby.
3.  Pertaining to place; it is improper near holy places, or holy persons such as one's guru.
4.  Pertaining to manner: unnatural methods of sexual intercourse are precluded.

Calling someone by animal names as a means of abuse, or hindering those who strive for an understanding of the dharma, are other causes for rebirth as an animal. Since you and all others have produced sufficient causes for this realm, to purify yourselves you should confess your faults with sincerity.

> From fear of the fire of suffering of the three lower realms, I go for refuge from the heart to the Triple Gem.
> Please grant your blessing to enable me to in-

tensely exert myself to accomplish all virtues and to abandon all non-virtues.

### d. HUMAN BEINGS

There are four great rivers of human suffering.

### (1) Birth

A baby endures great suffering in the mother's womb. It is constricted by the mother's organs as though trapped in a tight bag. When she moves, or drinks and eats anything excessively hot and cold, the baby experiences a sensation like that of falling off a cliff, and suffers considerable pain. At birth the "air of karma" expels him from the womb and he feels as if he is being buffeted between two huge mountains. Although the mother handles her baby with great care after birth and dresses him in soft clothes, he nevertheless feels as though his skin is being rubbed with sandpaper. All contact is painful, and because of this babies cry very much.

Ignorance, darkness and stupidity, which characterize children and remain even in adulthood, are the result of the period spent in the womb. Birth is the direct cause for sickness, old age and ultimately death.

### (2) Old age

Nobody desires to grow old. When old age comes the faculties of body and mind become weak. The knowledge of youth which was sharp as a knife turns rusty or is forgotten. Old people were also young once and all will eventually become like them. The process of ageing proceeds unnoticed but, were it to come suddenly, the suffering that it involves would be unbearable. Because it is a long and painful decline many old people simply wait for death to release them. Old age is a great obstacle for a person who wishes to begin the practice of dharma.

### (3) Sickness

When illness strikes, not only normal everyday activities are disrupted, but particularly the practice of dharma. From birth until death each person carries within himself the seeds of innumerable diseases, and when one of these is activated, troubles are experienced. The sufferings involved in sicknesses are clearly recognizable.

### (4) Death

You do not know what will happen tomorrow or what circumstances may arise. You can never be certain when you will die. Who can predict how and where he will die? All must endure the suffering of death. When it comes you will be far removed from the friends and relatives who surrounded you during life. No one can share the experience of death and no matter how close you were to your loved ones you must depart alone.

When you hear about the suffering of the hells you may remain unmoved, since it does not affect you directly, but when you hear about, and realize human suffering, you will be stirred by the truth of it.

### e. ASURAS

Jealousy is the principal cause for their misery, and it is mainly directed against the devas of the realm of desire who live in great splendor. The asuras are always engaged in battle against these devas. Even though there are lakes in which the families can see the fate of their warriors, still they continue to fight.

### f. DEVAS

The abandonment of the ten unskilful actions but without renunciation is the main cause for rebirth as a deva. Their lives are very long and their gratification is unlimited but, as their minds are totally dissipated by this round of pleasure, most devas have no thought for the dharma. Their life span seems to them very brief. When their skilful karma is exhausted, seven days (according to the reckoning of this realm) before their death they foresee their end and their place of rebirth. Their suffering is so intense that these seven days appear longer than all of their previous life. Their bodies lose their radiance, become dusty and begin to smell. Their garlands of flowers fade, they feel uncomfortable on their thrones and their friends desert them. At this time, because unskilful seeds of past karma appear, most devas are reborn in lower states. For this reason it is not desirable to be born as a deva and your goal should be complete liberation.

## 2. THE THREE KINDS OF MISERY

### a. THE MISERY OF MISERY

This is what ordinary people call suffering. All can recognize it whether or not they know about the dharma. It is the mental and physical misery endured in worldly existence.

### b. THE MISERY OF CHANGE

The misery of change is what people who lack the understanding of dharma mistake for real happiness. It includes all physical and mental pleasures. For example, a person who experiences the physical misery of discomfort in the shade seeks the warmth of a sunny spot. But, as soon as the heat of the sun becomes unpleasant, he moves into the shade. It is for this reason that it is called "the misery of change". Mental misery of this kind can be seen in the example of a people whose country has been liberated from an oppressor. Having obtained their freedom they rejoice, but eventually the situation turns into another form of oppression. Another example is the happiness of a man who has won a high position in society. If he remains in that position for a period of time, problems and difficulties will arise because of his responsibilities and due to competition from others. These will ultimately cause him and his relatives grief. All worldly people strive to acquire this kind of temporary happiness which in reality is only misery.

Why does it appear as happiness? Because this misery is less pronounced and less easy to perceive than the first kind described. If it was true happiness it would increase but instead it decreases and gradually turns into misery. When the misery of change is observed through the eye of the dharma it will be recognized to be one aspect of suffering, and the practice will have been worthwhile.

C. THE MISERY OF EXTENSIVENESS

It is the very fact of existence in samsara. Any rebirth, the basis for the first two kinds of misery, does not bring suffering only now, but is the instrument for the production of further unskilful actions, the fruits of which will undoubtedly ripen in the future. The pain felt from a sore on the hand is the first kind of misery, and all beings are aware of it. Those who have a good understanding of the dharma are aware of the second, but only aryas totally comprehend the third aspect of misery. If you rub a hair between the palms of your hands, you do not feel it, but aryas feel the misery of extensiveness in the same way as you would if that hair were in your eye.

All beings wish to escape from the first kind of misery; devas from the formless realms wish to escape from the second; and aryas desire freedom from the third.

Since every samsaric being is oppressed by the three types of misery you should now develop the wish to be liberated from samsara.

All unskilful deeds stem from four erroneous views. The belief that existence is permanent is the first error. Viewing this existence as happiness is the second. Believing the five aggregates to be pure when in fact the body is a mass of impurities and the mind is filled with defilements, is the third. To superimpose the idea of independent self-existence on all phenomena, while every existence is without self-nature, is the final misconception. If you fail to recognize these mistaken notions and to see how they are linked, your activities, like those of millions of other people, will be based on and fettered by them.

In dharma practice, there are two kinds of meditation: contemplation and concentration. By means of the former you develop intuitive understanding of impermanence, karma and its fruit, renunciation, the precious human form, interdependent origination, compassion, loving kindness, bodhichitta, as well as a relative understanding of shunyata. By means of the latter you achieve single-pointedness of mind. At the end of every contemplation you should concentrate on what has been realized. The mind, however, does not undergo development as a result of concentrated meditation alone. When practising dharma you must first understand as clearly as possible what you are learning. You must then comprehend what is to be accepted and abandoned, as well as the methods for destroying wrong conceptions. There are proper and improper times for the practice of contemplation. Since it is impossible to practise all the methods simultaneously, once you have found what is really effective for you, you should stop searching and concentrate on that. If energy decreases during meditation, then a brief contemplation on the benefits of meditation should help to overcome this feeling of sinking and build up further energy for concentration. In order to fell a tree you need to strike at the right spot (concentration) and to sharpen the axe well (contemplation). Afflictions are deeply rooted and are difficult to destroy immediately; therefore you must train yourselves to eradicate them gradually.

In order to end suffering, you must avoid its cause—the production of karma. To do this, you must find the method and put it into practice through your own efforts, because no meditator can transfer his insights to another person. The Buddha stated clearly that every being is, at the same time, his own master and his own enemy.

There are two steps for the destruction of karma:

1.  To purify the seeds of past unskilful karma which have the power to bear fruit.
2.  To prevent a fresh accumulation of unskilful karma. It is for these purposes that the extraordinary preliminaries are practised:

> Please grant your blessings that I may hold the banner of liberation by abandoning the view that this samsara, which is like an unbearable prison, is a delightful park, and by holding firmly the three trainings, the treasure house of the aryas.

## II. The Extraordinary Preliminaries

Dharma practice from the outset is a gradual process of mental development. When one practice becomes very powerful it leads naturally to the next. Therefore, without the experiences of the initial stages, it is impossible to achieve the final ones.

Nowadays, many people are interested in tantric practices but, to enter these with chances of success, it is necessary first to progress through other accomplishments which will lead onto the tantric path.

The specific requirements for tantra are the experiences of the Three Principles of the Path: a strong renunciation, bodhichitta and the correct view of sunyata. These experiences need to be stronger than those in the individual who follows the Paramitayana, in the manner that they act as a direct cause for the entry into the tantric path.

Other very important requirements include an indestructible faith in the Guru, such as explained in the *Lama Nga Chu Pa* (*Guru Pancashika, Fifty Verses on the Spiritual Teacher*), and the receiving of the proper initiation from a qualified master. Merely seeing the forms of divinities, reading tantric texts or knowing the mantras are not tantric practices. Even those who do not have any interest in the dharma can do this.

There are many different texts and ways of performing the extraordinary preliminaries, according to specific tantric practices. Here the general pattern of the preliminaries is shown, and to accomplish them you should keep in mind the necessity of meeting a spiritual teacher who will eventually reveal the details of the procedures.

A.  Taking refuge and generating bodhichitta

B.  Prostration
C.  Vajrasattva sadhana
D.  Offering the mandala
E.  Guru yoga

## A. *Taking Refuge and Generating Bodhichitta*

### 1. TAKING REFUGE

This is the most important preparation for the practice of dharma since it makes the mind serviceable for this purpose. A bowl in which food is to be served should be clean, a dirty bowl will spoil the food. Taking refuge in the Buddha is a necessary precondition for the successful practice of the Buddha dharma.

There are three divisions of taking refuge: (a) the object, (b) the reason and (c) the manner.

#### a. THE OBJECT

In everyday life a person who is powerless to solve a particular problem must seek the help and advice of someone who can assist him. Similarly, we go for refuge because we wish to be free from the misery of samsara and its causes, the bondage of karma and mental afflictions. To rely on those who are themselves powerless to assist is worthless since only the Buddha possesses all the proper qualifications.

Buddha in Tibetan is "Sang Gyas". "Sang" means awakened from the sleep of the two obstructions[8]; "Gyas" means the three qualities of a Buddha—compassion, wisdom and power—are fully developed. The Buddha's compassion is equal for all beings. His wisdom is unlimited and embraces all objects of knowledge. His power to rescue all beings is fully mature. These qualities of a Buddha can only be attained gradually with great perseverance by destroying all afflictions and perfecting all virtues. In everyday life also, a desired position can only be acquired by gradually accomplishing the prerequisites. On the Buddha's part all means of giving refuge are present. A person endowed with experience can advise others for he knows what must be avoided and what must be pursued. To offer help without experience is like guiding others when you yourself are blindfolded.

Just as all Buddhas have done, you also can achieve enlightenment because all beings have the seed of buddhahood. The Tibetan term is "Sang Gyas kyì Rig". "Rig" means seed or race. In some sutras this seed is called Buddha but you should not mistakenly assume that you have a Buddha inside you. Iron ore must go through many processes before the impurities are removed and it is refined. Similarly, you have the Buddha potentiality within, but it is shrouded in delusions. This seed can grow into perfect buddhahood by passing through many stages of purification.

Now, at the very beginning you cannot overcome all delusions at once. Continuous and persistent effort is the sole means by which you will eliminate them. All samsaric beings are temporarily separated from the Buddhas, but with the attainment of enlightenment they become of the same nature as all the Buddhas, just as rays of light from different sources focus and unite on one spot.

A meditation practised with a particular form of the Buddha is equivalent to worshipping all the Buddhas for their nature is one.

When taking refuge, visualize in the space directly before you the place of refuge as a pure land. In the centre is the wish-fulfilling tree adorned with the most precious objects imaginable; on the top of this tree is a large lotus seat surmounted by a golden throne; seated on it is the Root Guru in human form, surrounded by the line of gurus of the tradition. In front of him, also on a golden throne, stands Chakrasamvara and around him all the meditational deities. Buddha Shakyamuni attended by many Buddhas is seated on the right side of the guru while on his left is the bodhisattva Avalokiteshvara with a large retinue of bodhisattvas, arhats and pratyekabuddhas. All these are manifestations of the Guru. Behind the Guru on another throne is the Buddha's teaching in the form of scriptures. In the intermediate directions are dakas and dakinis, viras and viris and dharmapalas.

This is the visualisation according to this text, but if it is found to be too difficult, you can visualize your personal deity alone. The effect is the same whether you visualize a great assembly or just one Buddha.

b. THE REASON

There are two reasons for taking refuge:

i.   The will to be free from samsara. Unless you realize the misery of samsara neither this will nor the wish to take refuge can arise.
ii.  The trust in the Buddha as the sole help to accomplish this aim.

c. THE MANNER

The correct manner in which to take refuge is to entrust yourself to the Buddha with all sincerity. Without such an attitude of mind the circumambulation of stupas and recitation of verses are not so beneficial.

## 2. BODHICHITTA

When an individual with the initial or intermediate type of motivation takes refuge he desires to attain personal liberation from the suffering of samsara and its causes. Bodhichitta extends this desire to encompass all sentient beings. All beings in samsara share the same condition. Therefore, we aspire with enthusiasm to rescue them from this bondage and lead them to enlightenment. At present, we lack the necessary powers to accomplish this task but by attaining Buddhahood we can acquire them, not for our personal happiness but for the benefit of all living beings.

Bodhichitta is the wish for supreme enlightenment for the sake of others. The sign of true bodhichitta is the constant readiness to undergo any sacrifice for the happiness of all beings. Many instances of this are found in the former lives of the Buddha.

Sometimes, a similar willingness is felt, but this is not bodhichitta nor does it make us bodhisattvas. The pure bodhichitta grows gradually and our present state of mind is transformed only after long acquaintance with it. When bodhichitta arises spontaneously like the thought of food in a starving man, a person becomes a real bodhisattva. Then, the smallest virtuous action is incomparable with any ordinary good deed, creating merit as vast as space. Why is there such a profound difference? When the motivation for an action embraces all beings, the merit gained is of equal magnitude. When someone with an ordinary state of mind teaches with a benevolent intention he accrues as much merit as there are students in his classroom, but to teach with bodhichitta motivation accumulates merit beyond measure.

It is most important to arouse from within this wish to benefit others, for it shortens the path to buddhahood and is the root of all higher practices. For example, even if a shravaka meditates for a million years on shunyata, the merit gained will not equal that from one minute of similar meditation by a bodhisattva endowed with bodhichitta.

A disposition that is prepared to undergo hardships and accept the responsibility of helping all living beings single-handed gives rise to equanimity, the levelled terrain on which the waters of love and compassion may be poured. At present we feel close to those for whom we have attachment, and we dislike, or feel indifferent towards all others. Contemplation is absolutely essential for the development of an equanimity which has firm foundations, otherwise everyday worldly contacts will continue to disturb our equilibrium. bodhichitta is not something acquired instantaneously. It is similar to the process of building a house. The ground must first be levelled, and after the different materials have been collected and combined, construction can begin.

There are numerous ways of generating bodhichitta. The two main traditions are like two great rivers from a snowy mountain. Both originate from the Buddha Shakyamuni. One passed from Maitreya to Asanga and, through many gurus, to Atisha. The other from Manjushri to Nagarjuna, Shantideva and also to Atisha. Either can yield the same effect but if they are practised together the result is more powerful. The following methods is a combination of the two traditions.

There are eleven rounds of contemplation:

a. Equanimity.
b. Recognition of all beings as our mother.
c. Remembering their kindness.
d. Repaying their kindness.
e. Equality of self and others.
f. The faults of self-cherishing.
g. The advantages of cherishing others.
h. The mental attitude of exchanging the self with others.
i. Taking and giving.
j. The supreme wish.
k. Generation of bodhichitta.

These are the stations on the journey to bodhichitta. When making a journey, it is not enough merely to know the names of the stations; they must be recognized and a means found to reach them.

a. EQUANIMITY

First, we should develop an awareness of our general condition and our mental attitude. Then we must examine them to ascertain whether they are right or wrong.

*Examining our general condition*

Each of our activities is a combination of body and mind, yet when we search for the self that acts we cannot locate it physically in any part, not even in the smallest atom. Nor can we apprehend it even for the briefest moment in either our primary or secondary consciousness. When we try to discover the self, we tend to identify it with the body because it is visible and tangible. This leads to the assumption that when the body dies everything ceases and so the first misconception occurs. Those with somewhat more perception equate the mind, that controls all bodily actions, with the self. This is the second misconception. Superficially it appears to be so, but when analyzed and fully investigated, it will be found also untrue. The third erroneous view that arises from the failure to discover the self in either the body or the mind is the total negation of self. This is a grave error because sometimes this negation is mistaken for shunyata understanding and clung to with attachment. In this case there can be no progress but only regression since there does exist a relative self which meditates, which acts in daily life and which holds wrong views.

These are the main misunderstandings pertaining to the self but there are countless others. To arrive at the realization of shunyata we must cross many dangerous passes. Reading books will not lead there. It is extremely difficult to find in what manner the self really has existence. In order to discover the true nature of the relative self we must know the method of analysis well and acquaint ourselves with it. Then it will gradually become clearer to us. When first learning thangka painting we may know which color to put where but we do not know how to apply the pigment. We find that it is more difficult than we had thought. We must follow the master and accustom ourselves to the technique. It is exactly the same with meditation. The existence of the relative self is subtle and not gross or obvious as we assumed at the outset of our investigations.

## Our mental attitude

Someone who is doing intensive meditation does not need to rely on external circumstances for realization to occur, but in the beginning the analysis of the self can only be made on special occasions when the false self is manifest. At the time of experiencing strong emotions of hatred, suffering or happiness it appears clearly. However, it is not necessary to always rely on external stimuli, for such feelings arise in rapid succession from our thoughts alone. At such moments we must maintain lucid awareness and make a sharp examination of this appearance of the false self. In a situation where the pain in being the "I" which arises in the thought "I cannot bear this suffering" must be keenly scrutinized. What we will then find is a strong ego, an uncontrolled self that seems to stand independently of body and mind. Despite its vivid appearance, it is nothing but a creation of ignorance, a spurious fabrication based on the relative self, but without existence like the hallucination of a sick man. At such times we are particularly conscious of it, but at all times this deluded concept of the self is and has been with us. Until now we have given credence to this creation of our ignorance. We cling to the non-existent self and hold it very dear. A more easily apprehensible manifestation of it is our attitude of self-cherishing which arises from this deep-seated clinging. Those other beings who seem to help the self become "my family, my relatives, my friends, my compatriots", and we experience attachment to them. Of the many levels of beings there arise innumerable layers of attachment, like waves on the ocean. Countless unskilful deeds are thus produced for the false self and for those whom we consider as being on our side. Those who seem to harm us we call "enemy, our enemy's family, his friends, the other side". Towards them we have animosity. This constantly smouldering fire of hatred is directed both against the animate and the inanimate. For example, we feel annoyed and angry if we are planning to go out and it starts to rain. Thus more unskilful action is performed through the three doors of body, speech and mind. Yet a third section of beings exist for us. Because they seem totally unrelated to this self we cherish, we treat them with the indifference we accord to the stones on the road, neither rejoicing in their happiness nor caring for their sorrows.

We will discover this attitude in ourselves as well as in others, in groups, in nations, and even down to the smallest insect, for it has existed within us from beginningless time. As long as our behaviour conforms to these patterns we must examine it to see whether it is right or wrong. If, however, it does not, then we may rest, but we should be certain that our failure to discover these attitudes in ourselves is not due to our stupidity and inability to make a proper investigation. Everything we do is based on this, and therefore we have been oppressed by suffering which will continue both in our present and future lives so long as we fail to realize that this selfish approach to life is at fault. To produce a change in our attitude towards these three arbitrary categories of beings, we must create an internal revolution by means of the correct reason and proper methods.

Why do we have a special attachment to those whom we classify as our friends and which leads us to perform unskilful actions by sacrificing anything for their sake? Our reasons are nonsensical. We say that because they help us we must regard them in a special way. Although seemingly plausible, this is in fact a superficial and illogical reason; in previous lives these same beings have harmed us, frightened us, and devoured our flesh. Their very names have caused us to tremble and aroused our hatred. Until we are free from the cycle of samsara, they will again in future lives be our enemies and cause us harm. The temporary nature of our relationship with them can be clearly seen in this life, for a small disagreement is often enough to turn good friends into jealous enemies. It would be equally stupid to sacrifice everything for someone who has harmed us for many years just because he gave us some candy. The transformation of relations from good to bad is a frequently recurring phenomenon, not only among individuals but also among nations. When we train the mind, it is mostly unproductive to remember the harmful actions done to us by others but in this instance we must, since it will help to reduce our strong attachment and to diminish our conviction that these are permanent friends and helpers.

Why do we have the evil attitudes of killing, cheating, refusing help and wishing to harm those we classify as enemies? To feel obliged to hate those who harm us is equally superficial and senseless. Here, too, we should reject such reasoning. Our suffering is occasioned primarily by our personal karma, the fruits of which we are experiencing in the form of the harm done to us by others. At present they appear as enemies, but in the past they have shown us immeasurable kindness: so close was our relationship that our happiness was dependent on them. Until we become free from the wheel of samsara this situation of interdependence will continue. Even in this life our relationship with enemies is not permanent, for in a period of days, months or years our present enemy may become such a close friend that we will be willing to entrust him with our secrets. The political arena presents many examples of such changes in attitude. Someone may have been kind to us for many years, but if one day he scolds us and from that moment onwards we regard him as our chief enemy we are being extremely childish. Our hatred is pointless and we must make efforts to decrease aversion.

Why are we so indifferent to the great happiness enjoyed by some and the great misery undergone by others? Why do we feel that if no relationship has been established no reaction on our part is required? Although this may be true at present, these strangers have helped us in the past and will do so again in the future. Even now a few words are enough to establish a fruitful contact. Therefore, it is quite irrational to neglect and ignore them.

We must continue to reflect in these ways for many years and gradually we will succeed in destroying the polarity of our views, creating in their stead harmony and balance. Without this firm basis, a feeling of equality which can be generated rapidly is of a very transient nature. A drug can give temporary relief to someone who is extremely ill, but if the person requires surgery, this is the only treatment that will ultimately benefit him. Likewise, our negative emotions must be permitted to arise, then examined and surrendered to the scalpel of the correct attitude towards these three classes of beings.

If we are to build the palace of bodhichitta this is how we must prepare the ground. Mere knowledge about equanimity will not bring about change. Only through regular meditation will our attitude of gross distinctions and constant fluctuations between attachment and aversion gradually diminish. At the same time this will bring greater peace of mind which is obviously of great personal benefit. However, this is not our prime concern, since the main purpose of our practice is to develop a state of mind from which we can benefit all other beings.

Concentration on this first phase is of great importance. It takes time to effect real change; nevertheless, when following this method of the eleven rounds of contemplation each stage is practised from the outset.

> Please grant your blessings that I may generate
>     everlasting happiness in others
> For there is no difference between myself and
>     them;
> Never finding satisfaction from pleasures
> And not desiring even the slightest suffering.

b. RECOGNITION OF ALL BEINGS AS OUR MOTHER

The necessity of helping all other beings is not a gratuitous notion without valid foundation. Although at present other beings seem unrelated to us, we do in fact have a very close relationship with them, and therefore it is our responsibility to help them. The nature of this bond is that of mother and child. Our present existence is not a self-originated phenomenon but is the product of many former lives. In the past we have been born innumerable times through each of the four birth processes: from the womb, from an egg, from moisture, and by miracle. Birth from the womb or from an egg presupposes the presence of a mother; therefore, since we have taken birth by these two processes countless times, we must have had countless mothers. If we contemplate on this we will eventually realize that all beings have been our mother at some time.

It is extremely difficult to become persuaded of this because it requires conviction about rebirth and of the fact that we have been living for infinite time. Explanations alone will not furnish us with convincing proof. We must contemplate deeply, basing our reflection on the right reasons and acquiring, not intellectual understanding, but actual experience. Because this is such a difficult point many people hold the wrong view that there is only this life and that reincarnation does not exist. In order to develop firm conviction we must know the nature of consciousness, its existence and how it arises. If we never examine this, we will be spared many problems. Whereas through a sharp investigation, many different and often conflicting ideas about what constitutes mind and its function will emerge. If we can attain certainty as to the infinite number of our past lives then it will bring much force to our contemplation of regarding all beings as our mother.

When we see our mother of this life we experience instant recognition of her as such. Similarly when we can see whatever being we encounter as having been our mother, then we have accomplished this stage. We must take many different beings as examples and try to feel about them in this way. Gradually we will develop this ability until finally we will be able to regard our mother and a dog in the same light. In this life we are the child of a human mother. In the past we have been the puppy of a bitch. There is no difference for the relationship has always been that of mother and child. The training of the mind to perceive this link between ourselves and other beings is the practice of seeing all beings as our mother. Qualitatively there is a great difference between this and the practice of equanimity. While the latter cultivates peace of mind, the former fosters closeness and a feeling of relatedness. A plain at sunrise is evenly lit although not yet warmed. Then, as the sun rises higher, the heat increases. This stage of practice is like the sun-rise and the stages that follow are like the growing heat as the sun reaches its zenith.

## c. REMEMBERING THEIR KINDNESS

Mere recognition of all beings as our mother is insufficient because we must also remember their kindness. If we contemplate our own mother's kindness towards us our fondness for her will grow. Before our birth we were protected and preciously carried in her womb. We were in a state of total helplessness and complete dependence. Our presence there was not only a great physical burden to her but was also a responsibility curtailing her freedom of action. When eating, walking, sitting or sleeping, she was constrained to be mindful of our presence and welfare. This she did joyfully. At birth, we gave great suffering to our mother yet she forgot this at once and rejoiced as though she had found a precious gem. We had no control over our physical functions, yet she felt no revulsion towards our vomit or excretions and cared for us gently. When she looked at us and spoke our name she did so in a special way. Her tenderness was not in response to some kindness we had shown her but was the result of her enormous compassion. She has helped us in countless ways, and it is due to her kindness that we have reached our present state of development.

We may argue that it was her duty to care for us but we should reflect on the nature of this care, the spontaneous gladness with which she accepted the burden of our existence. Without her constant attention we would not be alive now. She did so not in the hope of repayment nor because she was compelled to do so. She had freedom to choose and her choice was to benefit us. Our mother may at times show a self-cherishing attitude but ultimately, when it is a question of her personal benefit and ours, she sacrifices her own benefit and well-being.

A serious practice of dharma is not confined merely to the human sphere but encompasses all living creatures and the manner of their being. The love and the care of a human mother for her child is also observed among animals. Fledglings are helpless and their parents are not very strong either, but if the nest is attacked the parents will defend their brood selflessly and will often die in the process.

As a result of particular karmic relations from the past, there are cases of mothers who maltreat their offspring but this is the exception. Universally, the attitude of mother to child is one of love. Since we are attempting to cultivate our minds we must always consider positive aspects. By dwelling on kindness our mind develops in such a way that we become able to benefit others. Nothing is gained by dwelling on negative aspects. To think about the harm other beings do to us when we are not in the mother/child relationship is to pursue a wrong path. Such physical or mental suffering is the result of our karma, and those particular beings who inflict it are merely instruments of its accomplishment. The kindness we experience at the hands of others far outweighs the harm inflicted on us.

Since we are samsaric beings we have taken innumerable births. To alleviate the sufferings of these lives and to acquire happiness we always depend on countless beings because we have never been able to achieve this ourselves. Until by our own efforts we end the cycle of samsara in ourselves, we will continue in our future lives to follow this same pattern of dependence on others.

With the help of sentient beings we have come halfway between the higher and lower realms. To complete the journey to enlightenment we will continue to rely on the assistance and friendship of these good companions who have stood by us in the past. Our food and shelter, our clothes and the money we use all come to us by virtue of their kindness. Whatever their motivation is in providing us with these necessities or luxuries, the end product is our benefit. Our constant desire is for increasing happiness. We long to hear what is pleasant and gives us joy but not that which causes us distress. We wish for fame and praise either directly or indirectly. Who can grant us these other than our fellow beings? Their benevolence is essential for our samsaric contentment but more than that, without them all spiritual attainment is impossible. How can there be the practice of the Six Perfections without sentient beings as our object? To reach Budhahood we rely both on the Buddha's kindness in showing the teaching we follow and the assistance of sentient beings.

In the *Bodhisattvacaryavatara* the Bodhisattva Shantideva points out that

> Although both the Buddha and all beings are
>     equally important for our attainment of Bud-
>     dhahood,
> We respect, worship and make offerings to the
>     Buddha but neglect sentient beings.
> What kind of attitude is this?

We should therefore develop a feeling of gratitude towards both and become conscious of our bond. If a poor man is given a sack of grain by one man and a field by another, who has been kinder to him? Both are equally kind. The Buddha has given us the dharma seed and the beings are the field in which we must plant and tend that seed.

d. REPAYING THEIR KINDNESS

Having realized that we owe a debt of gratitude, we must find out how it can be repaid. Since all beings wish to be rid of suffering and to gain happiness, we must recognize their problems and attempt to remove them while granting what they desire. Our usual way of practising dharma is like a ray of sunshine filtering through a small hole but the bodhisattva's practice is like sunlight flooding the whole land. We must effect a total change of consciousness.

> Please grant your blessings that I may generate
>   effortless compassion
> Just as a mother's love for her wayward son,
> By thinking again and again how those tormented
>   beings, my mothers, have been kind to me.

### e. EQUALITY OF SELF AND OTHERS

We should understand how the will to repay the kindness of motherly sentient beings leads to those new attitude of mind. How can we help them? We must learn to separate them from what they have but do not want, namely, their suffering; we must give them what they do not have but desire—happiness. We must find the strength necessary to shoulder this responsibility and we must develop the conviction that we are able to do so personally. We may see clearly the desirability of eliminating our own suffering but question the necessity of removing that of others. The practice of this stage of the meditation is aimed precisely at persuading us of this point.

If we take ourselves as an example, we can see our reluctance to accept even the smallest degree of suffering. This sentiment is echoed by all beings. From our own experiences we know that we constantly desire greater happiness no matter how much we get. Just like ourselves, other beings too are dissatisfied and crave greater satisfaction. Not only do we and they lack transcendental bliss, but even the samsaric happiness we enjoy is limited. The practice of skilful action produces happiness yet we shun this like poison. Although we detest suffering we must endure many kinds; the suffering of physical pain, the suffering of change and the suffering of extensiveness. We cling to suffering, the result of unskilful deeds which we pursue like dogs after meat.

We and other sentient beings share the same thoughts and mental attitudes. Our mental and physical suffering are alike, as is our pursuit of unskilful action. In this respect we are like images cast from the same mould and, since our condition is identical, to think only of ourselves is unreasonable and cannot be substantiated. The arguments that apply to our need for happiness are exactly those that apply to all sentient beings, therefore there are good reasons to care for others as we do for ourselves.

If we see the importance of eliminating our own suffering but, feeling unaffected by the suffering of others we do not see the pressing need to eliminate it, we should consider this example from the *Bodhisattvacaryavatara* by Shantideva;

> If the leg is cut, is it true that the hand does not
> need to tend the wound because only the leg has
> sustained the injury? Since the person as a whole
> experiences the suffering, it is natural for the hand,
> although not affected, to take action.

In the same way we should feel responsible for helping others.

A farmer sows wheat in order to harvest the grain and not for the stalks or leaves which, although they are side-products, can be useful to him. In the same way, we should benefit others with a pure motivation and not for the side-effect of self-benefit which will eventually arise. We may doubt the truth of this on the grounds that the beneficial results of our actions are not immediately perceptible, although we are quite willing to save money for our old age despite the fact that we derive no immediate benefit from this. We feel justified in doing so because we envisage a definite period in the future when our efforts will bear fruit. To accept the latter as logical while rejecting the former is short-sighted, for if the results of our benevolent actions towards other beings are experienced in another life, this is just as much part of the continuum as the change from youth to old age.

True realization of the equality of self and others comes only after years of practice. The reasons for helping others are manifold. We must know how to dispel the doubts that arise in our mind, dealing with them in a real way and not in a theoretical manner.

> Please grant your blessings that I may attain the power of equalizing myself with others,

> With the mind which discriminates between the shortcomings of working for oneself and the Buddha's virtuous actions, solely benefiting others.

### f. THE FAULTS OF SELF-CHERISHING

All beings without exception should be deemed as precious as ourselves. Although we may pay lip service to this we cling to the self-cherishing attitude. For example, we are not particularly anxious if a dog is left outside during a downpour, but if we have to venture out we feel most perturbed. We persist in regarding ourselves as most precious while others seem less important. Whenever feelings like this arise we must immediately change our attitude by deciding that if one being must suffer neglect it will be oneself rather than the other. This does not imply that we should adopt an extreme attitude of self-neglect, for this will neither help us nor others.

Buddha has stated that the self-cherishing attitude is like a chronic disease which brings many other kinds of suffering in its wake. This prevents us not only from achieving our goals but also from making any headway since we are always preoccupied with ourselves. All beings from the lowest hells to the highest bodhisattvas, hindered from their attainment of buddhahood by the imprints of afflictions, are fettered by the self-cherishing attitude, the root of all troubles. Two insects fighting or two nations at war clearly reveal the many disadvantages of this harmful attitude. Although it seems to help us temporarily it is actually the greatest obstacle to true bodhisattva practice. Through greed and desire to satisfy the self or through aversion and our efforts to avoid what displeases the self, we accumulate countless unskilful deeds.

Our innate attitude has always been to deem ourselves of supreme importance. This view must be totally reversed.

> Please grant your blessings that I may destroy the
> great demon of self-cherishing by holding it as
> a spiteful object
> And by seeing this chronic disease which grasps
> oneself dearly as the originator of all undesired
> suffering.

g. THE ADVANTAGES OF CHERISHING OTHERS

The cultivation of this attitude is right and worthwhile. The supreme qualities of enlightened beings as well as the brief worldly happiness we enjoy result from our efforts for the well-being of our fellow creatures. This precious human form with which we are at present endowed is the result of our attempts to practise non-violence and to refrain from killing and harming. Our possessions and living facilities are the result of our practice of charity and other skilful deeds. All spiritual attainments stem from our ability to cherish others. When Buddha turned the Wheel of the Dharma after his enlightenment it was because of his great compassion for all sentient beings. At all stages of our practice, at the beginning, middle and end when the supreme goal has been achieved, cherishing others is of utmost importance. We can observe that animals such as dogs, birds and mice feel attraction for a person who is kind to them and feeds them, but shy away from those who lack gentleness and are rough. A person who really cherishes all beings, not just his friends and relatives, is praised and respected by others who regard him as having a noble character.

Cherishing kind people is easy for everybody, both those who practise dharma and those who do not. What is especially difficult is to cherish those of unpleasant nature to whom we feel averse. Soldiers train so that when they go into battle they are well prepared; an untrained soldier is useless. Similarly, we must prepare ourselves to meet unfavorable situations, and be ready to deal with awkward people. By realizing that others neglect them we should treat them with even greater compassion. When we help someone who does not respond with the gratitude we expect, we should not feel discouraged but should recognize that such a person is in fact our teacher. He allows us to measure how far we have developed in our bodhichitta conduct by presenting us with a situation that tests our qualities. It is also possible that the Buddha or our own Guru may sometimes manifest in such beings. Since we usually sit in our room and meditate on the advantages of cherishing others, it is difficult to evaluate if real changes in our attitude have occurred. If, under such unfortunate circumstances we are capable of reacting without getting upset, we can see that some genuine progress has been made. On the other hand, when we realize that we lack sufficient equanimity to deal with these situations, it spurs us on to greater efforts. We have the other person to thank for this incentive. Nations test their bombs and if they prove defective, they continue their efforts to develop more efficient arms. Cherishing others is our weapon against the self-cherishing attitude. Our external enemies will die whether or not we bring about their destruction, but our fiercest enemy, the one within, will not die unless we wage war. If we know how to think deeply and practise sincerely, these teachings can truly be of help to us in bad times.

Change will only come gradually after years of practice because our self-cherishing attitude is so deeply rooted that it seems part and parcel of our human nature. Men fight if someone trespasses on their territory, yet we harbor a far more harmful intruder but show no concern over its presence. In this old body we must grow a new mind, for change will only occur in this way.

h. THE MENTAL ATTITUDE OF EXCHANGING THE SELF WITH OTHERS

When we have become fully aware of the disadvantages of cherishing ourselves at the expense of others, and of the advantages of cherishing all beings above ourselves, we must begin the actual practice of exchange of self with others. This does not mean that we become others or that they become us, but that we change our attitude at the most fundamental level. Although we are quite unaccustomed to this new attitude, it is possible with efforts to effect a transformation so that when another being suffers we cannot bear his anguish and suffer also. We can similarly experience true joy at the happiness of others. A mother feels greater suffering when her child is in pain than if she were actually suffering herself. She also feels great happiness when she knows her child is contented, because she holds her child more precious than herself. Her ability of exchange is limited to one being but our aim is to extend it to all beings.

> Please grant your blessings that I may hold as dear as my life those sentient beings who even rise as enemies against me, by seeing that the gateway to the birth of infinite virtues is the mind whose prime concern is to cherish all mothers and sentient beings.

i. TAKING AND GIVING

We begin this meditation by imagining the wrong self-cherishing attitude in the form of a black spot at our heart.

Around us are the sentient beings of the six realms. We can visualize them in their respective realms or all in human form. Then we begin to generate compassion, the strong wish to separate the greatly suffering beings from their misery.

Breathing in slowly through the nostrils, we visualize the mental and physical suffering of all beings entering our body in the form of black rays which are absorbed into the black spot of self-cherishing at the heart. As we do this we imagine that all beings are left pure and bright and that our self-cherishing attitude must bear all this suffering as punishment.

Then, realizing that all beings seek happiness but lack it, we generate loving kindness and the willingness to give away our happiness.

We then visualize all the merits and seeds of our skilful deeds in the form of a radiant white light which, while exhaling, radiates from our nostrils embracing all sentient beings. As it touches them, it gives mental and physical happiness.

At the beginning it is very important to persevere as long as is necessary with achieving clarity in the visualization before we actually start to inhale the suffering and exhale the happiness. Through acquaintance it will be possible to begin at this stage immediately. We may visualize all types of beings in human form as weak and poor while they suffer, then later in the meditation as happy and content. We see them as from a tower, which enables us to have an overall view of all beings around us.

Next we reflect on the suffering of lack of material happiness of sentient beings and their desire and expectations for material comfort. Again we inhale their misery and exhale loving kindness and light, thus satisfying all their needs.

Recognizing their great ignorance and the suffering they endure through not knowing the dharma, we accept this burden and send out light in the form of wisdom so that they become like Buddhas, freed of their ignorance and supremely wise.

If this practice is done well, the quality of our inhalations and exhalations becomes vastly different from the anapanasati type of breathing awareness.

We may question the usefulness of this practice since we seem to be helping beings in imagination only. It is, however, greatly effective for the development of energy. It brings us closer to genuine bodhichitta and help us to accumulate great virtue. With a pure intention we develop very much from one breath to another. It is like furnishing the beings with the guarantee that sooner or later we will really be able to alleviate their suffering and grant them happiness. This is the preparation we must make to achieve our goal.

In the same way that if we have a dirty pot we must clean it first before putting something into it, we must take the suffering of sentient beings from them before we can give them happiness. As we take on the suffering and it is absorbed, the black spot of the self-cherishing attitude diminishes and finally disappears, just as a black cloud gradually disperses and dissolves into space. At the end of this part of the meditation, we imagine that all beings have much happiness and with a joyful mind we spend some time in concentration on this.

> I understand that the self-cherishing attitude does
>     not lead anywhere,
> And that the way of the Buddhas is to cherish
>     others more than anything else.
> I request the Venerable Compassionate Gurus to
>     bless me that I may be able to take on myself at
>     this very moment all the suffering, seeds of non-
>     virtue and obstacles of all sentient beings, my
>     mothers,
> And to give them all my happiness and virtues.

j. THE SUPREME WISH

When we look to see if sentient beings really do have this happiness, we find that what we have done in our visualization has not affected them directly but has helped us to develop the supreme wish. This must act as a stimulus to increase our efforts and, by reflecting on the kindness of all beings and their poor condition, we must decide with stronger love and compassion that we alone will accept the responsibility of really delivering them from their suffering. Since we ourselves have accepted their kindness, why should we leave it to someone else to make the repayment? We should feel that beings look to us alone for the fulfilment of their hopes. Formerly we have voiced the wish to help others but we firmly decide to undertake this task single-handed. This has arisen through a series of stages called examination meditations. The more profound and thorough this analysis has been, the stronger will be the formal meditation on the pure wish.

## K. THE GENERATION OF BODHICHITTA

After arising from the former meditation, we must examine ourselves to see if it is really in our capabilities to fulfil the commitment we have made. We shall find that although we aspire to rid ourselves and others of suffering, we and they are totally overwhelmed by it. Even great arhats who are able to do much to help beings do not have complete power. Even great bodhisattvas, whose compassion for beings is immense, are unable to act without the help of the Buddhas. The only beings who are all-powerful and utterly independent in their ability to give help are the Buddhas.

At present our consciousness is like the sun obscured by clouds. As the clouds disperse the sunshine becomes brighter until finally the sun floods the whole land with its brilliant and radiant light. In the same way at each of the bodhisattva stages certain obstacles are eliminated and the power of wisdom grows stronger. When all obstacles have been abandoned and wisdom is fully developed one becomes an enlightened being, a Buddha.

A Buddha's wisdom, like the unobstructed light of the

sun, penetrates all knowable objects or dharmas with equal intensity. Because a Buddha is endowed with such wisdom he sees clearly how beings may be liberated. However, an enlightened one not only has wisdom but also has great compassion which means that he never relaxes but works unceasingly for the welfare of all sentient beings. This great compassion binds him to them yet he is free from their sufferings; it is a million times stronger than that of the bodhisattvas whose compassion is immense, and causes him never to neglect a being as we so often do.

In addition to his all-encompassing wisdom and great compassion, he has the power of completely effective action. He is always ready and is never forgetful. However, just as the brilliant light of an unclouded noonday sun cannot shine into a pot that is turned upside down, so the Buddha's help cannot reach us if we are not ready.

Thus, we can see that only by becoming a Buddha and attaining these superior qualities will it be possible to accomplish fully what we desire for ourselves and others. When the strong will to reach full enlightenment for the sake of all motherly sentient beings is of the nature of our mind, this is bodhichitta. To generate this once is not bodhichitta and does not make us a bodhisattva. Only after many years of practice can this frame of mind become habitual. Then the will to liberate all beings arises spontaneously whenever we see them suffering. At that time the mind is pure bodhichitta and one is a bodhisattva, having attained the first of the five Mahayana paths.

We cannot rest content with this achievement for bodhichitta is the steadfast vow not to rest until buddhahood is reached. When this vow has been taken, we must follow resolutely every practice necessary for its fulfilment. If there is a hidden treasure at the top of a mountain, the wish to unearth it is not enough one must take action, climb the mountain and start digging. Buddhahood is within everyone's reach, since all have the necessary potential. All dharmas have void nature and it is precisely because the mind also has void nature that enlightenment is attainable. To say that Buddhahood is beyond our reach is a complete contradiction. Before we have iron we have the unrefined ore; to transform this requires knowledge and skill. In the same way our everyday mind, which is like a seed, can be metamorphosed into enlightened mind.

If it is our sincere wish to develop bodhichitta this is how we must practise.

> May the precious and supreme bodhichitta
> Grow where it has not grown;
> May it unceasingly increase
> Where it has already grown and is undefiled.

## 3. THE TRAINING OF THE MIND

Outside the meditation period there is the need to actualize the experience in one's daily life. There are numerous points with respect to this training, and they have been summarized by the Khadam Geshe Che Ka Wa in seven divisions:

a.  Explanation of the basis for the Training of the Mind.
b.  Actual generation of bodhichitta.
c.  Being able to turn all unfavorable circumstances into the pure practice of bodhichitta.
d.  The practice for one life condensed into five forces.
e.  The measure of the development of bodhichitta.
f.  Eighteen commitments of the Training of the Mind.
g.  Advice on the Training of the Mind.

a.  In order to develop bodhichitta we need a firm basis in the meditations on impermanence, the precious human rebirth, and so forth, as explained above.

b.  There are two types of bodhichitta:

1.  Conventional: compassion and love.
2.  Absolute: the realization of voidness.

c.   In times of sickness we should feel that it is the result of our past karma, and we should pray that this suffering be sufficient to alleviate the suffering of all sentient beings. Also, when experiencing happiness and wealth, we should not forget bodhichitta practice.

d.   The five forces are as follows:

1.   The force of beneficial intention. From today until the attainment of buddhahood, all good motivations will be combined into one, bodhichitta. This sets your intention on the development of bodhichitta from the time you wake up.

2.   The force of acquaintance. Whatever you do or think or say becomes a means for the development of bodhichitta.

3.   The force of the white seed. Whatever virtuous actions you do, always direct these towards the development of bodhichitta.

4.   The force of uneasiness and disgust whenever the self-cherishing attitude arises.

5.   The force of prayers. Pray that you will never be separated from the mind that wishes to develop bodhichitta.

e.   Whether you are meditating or not, thinking of bodhichitta or not, if you have a natural effortless love and compassion for all beings in all circumstances, this is the measure of your development of bodhichitta. The naturalness is like that of a person who has achieved the perfection of patience or like that of an accomplished horseman.

f.   The eighteen commitments.

1.   Do not transgress the vows of the Training of the Mind. To despise the Hinayana, for example, would be to transgress the foundation of the bodhichitta practice.

2.   Do not transgress vowed conduct by doing such things as digging earth, cutting down trees, or any acts which disturb the lives of any sentient being. You must always act out of consideration for all beings.

3.  Do not be one-sided in the dedication of your bodhichitta practice. Thus, you should not practise bodhichitta only in relation to your relatives or friends. You must not exclude any being from your practice.

4.  Do not ostentatiously change your outer actions because of an inner change of mind. If others are eating, do not break company and sit in meditation.

5.  Do not say bad and abusive things about any sentient being. You can never be certain whether a being is a bodhisattva or not, and harsh words to a bodhisattva destroy your chances for a higher rebirth.

6.  Do not look for faults in others or dwell on what faults you see. You should rather see how you too share in these faults. "To see your own faults is wisdom, to leave the fault of others in indifference is virtue."

7.  Observe yourself and recognize your most serious affliction, and you should attend to that one first.

8.  Abandon all hopes for the good results of your actions. You should have the pure selfless motivation of helping all sentient beings.

9.  Do not mix the poison of ego-grasping, self-cherishing, or the belief in independent self existence, with the pure practice of bodhichitta. This is like destroying good food by adding poison to it.

10. Do not hold a grudge against those who harm you. Harbor no revenge motives nor return any acts of harm.

11. Take abusive words, without retaliating in kind; exert patience at all times.

12. Do not be indulgent with your afflictions.

13. Do not spitefully cause suffering to others by sharp words.

14. When you do something bad, do not pretend someone else did it by shifting the blame. Also, do not burden others with your own responsibility and work-load.

15. Do not be possessive and use the wealth and achievements of others for your own; even thinking to do so is a violation of your training.

16. Do not think to develop bodhichitta to be protected from evil circumstances such as harmful spirits. Your motivation should only be to help other sentient beings.

17. Abandon pride and a sense of accomplishment from the practice of bodhichitta.

18. Abandon thoughts of having another suffer so that you will be happy. This would be like the heir apparent wishing the king to die.

g. Advice on the Training of the Mind.

1. There are many yogas for all types of mundane actions. Whatever you do, from the time you wake up, you should do with a selfless attitude in order to benefit all sentient beings. Since, by doing bodhichitta practice you have given up yourself for others, when you eat you should think, "I am eating in order to survive to help all sentient beings." When you turn the light off think, "Now the door to lower rebirths is closed." The same attitude should prevail for all daily actions.

2. Whatever mantras you might think to use to eliminate the harmful interferences from others, think rather on the bodhichitta exchange of self for others, and return loving kindness.

3. Whatever virtuous actions you do should begin with the bodhichitta motivation and end with the dedication of merit for your own and all others' enlightenment. On waking, think, "Whatever I may do today, may it be for all sentient beings." On going to sleep, count not your money like a trader, but count your virtuous actions and apply opponent powers to any non-virtuous action committed.

4. Remain indifferent to all sorts of living conditions, not letting them interfere with your practice of training the mind. When ill, think, "May the sufferings I am now experiencing be sufficient for the suffering of all sentient beings." When happy do not be carried away so that

you forget dharma, rather think, "The happiness I am now experiencing has karmic causes, therefore I must collect the white karmic causes for future happiness."

5. Keep all vows in general pure, and especially the commitments of the Training of the Mind.

6. Whenever you commit non-virtuous actions, grasp the Four Opponent Powers and, clearly seeing their consequences, try not to commit such actions in the future.

There are three difficulties for the abandonment of the afflictions:

    i. It is difficult to recognize the afflictions.

    ii. Even if recognized, it is difficult to apply the Four Opponent Powers;

    iii. It is difficult to cut the continuum of the afflictions.

7. Gather the favorable circumstances for dharma practice.

    i. Find a spiritual teacher.

    ii. Develop and tame your mind.

    iii. Gather the necessary food and clothing.

8. Meditate on the three non-decreasing attitudes.

    i. Do not lose faith in the spiritual master.

    ii. Do not lose interest in the Training of the Mind.

    iii. Do not lose the practice of pure sila.

9. Never separate your own action of body, speech and mind from virtuous actions.

10. Develop an unbiased attitude towards all sentient beings without being selective.

11. Direct all your thoughts, whatever comes into your imagination, towards the Training of the Mind.

12. Develop mercy and compassion and an awareness of the arisal of afflictions especially for those who are close

to you, since anger and irritation have more opportunity to manifest where there is frequent contact.

13. Follow the practice of the Training of the Mind no matter what your living conditions may be. You should not be a fair weather meditator, practising only while the sun shines and you feel well.

14. Condense the practice of the dharma by developing bodhichitta through exchange of self and others, and have more regard for the next life than for the present one.

15. For some people, doing dharma practice is a cause of drowsiness while in doing worldly actions they expend energy. There are six reversed actions to be abandoned:

    i. Reversed patience, for worldly matters and no patience for difficulties in dharma practice.

    ii. Reversed taste, for warfare and trade and no taste for dharma practice.

    iii. Reversed mercy, for the poor dharma practitioners instead of for rich samsaric-drenched people.

    iv. Reversed wish or intention, for worldly pleasures and not for insights into dharma.

    v. Reversed generosity, giving money or samsaric allurements instead of giving teaching in the dharma.

    vi. Reversed rejoicing, in the sufferings and non-virtues of your enemies instead of in your own and others' virtuous actions. Geshe Potowa has said that this non-virtuous action of rejoicing in the non-virtues of others is worse than others' non-virtuous actions.

16. Follow a steady practice of dharma. Do not practise while only in a spiritual atmosphere; it is important to have self-discipline in your practice even while away from a conducive environment.

17. Your practice of the Training of the Mind should be done

single-pointedly, without any external, distracting considerations.

18. Make special efforts to abandon afflictions by always being alert for them. The forces of afflictions are not inherently strong for, once the appropriate opponents are located, they can be overcome.

19. Abandon boasting while you are helping others. It is your duty to help others, so you should be grateful when such opportunity arises.

20. Abandon holding a grudge, or becoming angry when being criticized in front of people. You should be able to control your attitude when faced with abuse or with annoying circumstances.

21. Do not practise dharma in an ostentatious way in order to gain a good reputation.

22. Do not be inconsistent by leaving a practice for another time but do your dharma practice until you attain actual experience.

## B. Prostration

Prostration can be practised to the object of refuge or as part of the Guru Yoga. It is one of the best methods for purifying the seeds of unskilful karma, particularly of physical karma. It is effective against karmic obstacles, afflictions, and especially counteracts pride. The meaning of the Tibetan term "chak tshal" is "requesting the hand"; we request to be given what is in the Buddha's hand, his virtuous qualities of body, speech and mind.

There are two methods of prostration involving either three or four centres. In one, we touch the crown of the head, the forehead, the neck and the chest; in the other, simply the crown, the neck and the chest are touched, and this is also considered sufficient.

If we do prostrations by touching three points, then the crown symbolises our desire to attain the Buddha's body, the neck, his speech and the chest, his mind. To obtain these three, we must master Wisdom and Means, both inseparably united. As we touch the three centres, our hands symbolise this. There are different ways of joining the palms, but in the Mahayana tradition the thumbs are tucked in, in the gem-holding gesture.

We may prostrate either by placing only the knees, forehead and palms on the ground, or by making a full prostration in which the whole body touches the ground and the arms are outstretched. If there is sufficient space it is always better to perform full prostrations in which case it is important to rise quickly. The correct time to rest when making prostrations is after rising and not when one is on the ground. As in all things, we should take care to follow the proper procedure because the consequences of knowing a rule yet transgressing it are serious. In this case, to rest on the ground out of laziness may result in an unfortunate rebirth. On rising, the palms should be flat on the ground. Using the knuckles as a means of support shows disrespect towards the object of prostration because it is lazy and may result in rebirth as an animal with hooves. Prostration if practised incorrectly is harmful, just as food which is meant for our nourishment if wrongly used can be a cause of death.

The performance of full prostrations is more beneficial since the merit accumulated equals the atoms in the earth beneath the outstretched body. If they are done correctly with the proper intention, then the merit acquired may result in rebirth as a Chakravartin king. In the *Manjushrivikridittsutra* taught by the Buddha to Manjushri, the benefit of skilful prostrations and the bad effects of unskilful ones are discussed in great detail. Since prostrations are a powerful means of creating merit, we may infer that our failure to enjoy their potential effects is caused either by our incorrect practice or by a strong manifestation of afflictions which counteracts the seeds of skilful karma. In the sutra given by the Buddha to Manjusri, he mentions hatred as being the

most destructive of all afflictions since it annihilates all skilful karma that has been accumulated.

When making prostrations, we should recite the
*Triskandhasutra*, a form of confession which mentions the
names of thirty-five Tathagatas and the ways in which we
transgress the Buddha's teaching. It takes about forty prostrations to complete on recitation after which one begins
again. The body makes the physical movements, by repeat-
ing the sutra we make prostration of speech, and our deep
respect towards the object of refuge constitutes mental prostration. If we practise in this way, we make prostration
through all three doors and not merely with the body.

It is wise to begin with fifty prostrations gradually increasing to one hundred, then to one hundred and fifty, and
so forth. Otherwise the only result will be exhaustion which
is not the intended purpose.

## C. Vajrasattva Sadhana

This sadhana is different from the one given in Padma
Karpo's text which explains a visualisation with the consort
and, since this requires initiation, it has not been described
here.

On the crown of one's head, visualise a lotus seat. Rest-
ing on this is a luminous moon-disc on which is seated
Vajrasattva, the form of all the Buddhas, facing in the same
direction as oneself. He is the manifestation of the Buddha's
power of purification and his radiant pure white colour
symbolises the Buddha's purity. He has one face and two
hands. In the right hand he holds the vajra which signifies
upaya, great compassion, and in the left he holds the bell
representing prajna, great wisdom which, like the two wings
of a bird, must work in unison for the attainment of enlightenment. He is adorned with beautiful ornaments and clad
in silken garments. To symbolise his energy and power of
action, his appearance is youthful and dynamic. Seated in
the vajra posture, he looks down upon one with compas-

sion. Having made this visualisation, one takes Refuge, generates the bodhichitta, and the first six verses of the Seven Limb Puja are recited, the dedication of merit being left until the end.

### (1) The refuge and generation of bodhichitta

I go for refuge to the Buddha, the Dharma and the Supreme Community until the attainment of enlightenment. By the merit gained from my practice of generosity and other perfections, may I attain the state of a Buddha for the sake of all sentient beings.

### (2) Prostrations

As many atoms as there are in the thousand million worlds, so many times do I make reverent salutation to all the Buddhas of the three times, to the Dharma, to the Excellent Community. I pay homage to all the shrines and places where the bodhisattvas have been and make profound obeisance to the Teachers.

### (3) Offerings

Just as Manjusri and other bodhisattvas make offerings to the enlightened beings, so do I make offerings to the Buddhas and bodhisattvas so that I may develop the bodhichitta.

### (4) Confession

In this beginningless samsaric state, in this life and in other lives, I have committed unfitting and unskilful actions or caused others to do so. Being confused by ignorance, I have even taken pleasure and rejoice in these non-virtuous actions. By confessing this to all the Buddhas and Bodhisattvas with a pure state of mind, I open my heart and expose all my faults, applying the Four Opponent Powers. The harmful mistakes which I have committed through ignorance and foolishness, mistakes in the world of everyday experience as well as in understanding and intelligence, all these I admit to the enlightened beings. What is not good, O Buddhas, I will not do again.

### (5) Rejoicing

I rejoice in the compassionate deed of giving happiness to sentient beings. I rejoice in the deeds of the Buddhas and bodhisattvas in granting peace to sentient beings. I rejoice in their ocean-like wish to give permanent happiness to all beings.

### (6) Requesting the Buddhas to turn the Wheel of the Dharma

Saluting them with folded hands, I entreat the Buddhas in all the quarters to light the lamp of the dharma for those obscured by the darkness of suffering.

### (7) Requesting for stability of the Buddha's physical manifestations

With hands folded in reverence, I implore the Buddhas desiring to enter parinirvana to remain here for endless ages so that life in this world does not grow dark.

Then, the white letter HUM appears on a luminous moon-disc in the heart of Vajrasattva. The white letters of the mantra stand clockwise around the HUM, and from each syllable flows a fountain of nectar. Each produces its own sound and radiates light. At this stage, we make the following request:

O Bhagavat Vajrasattva, I request you to purify and cleanse myself and all sentient beings of our harmful deeds, our afflictions, and the transgressions we have committed against our vows.

When this request has been made, the HUM in Vajrasattva's heart emits rays of light which wash away the harmful deeds and delusions of all sentient beings who then make offerings which delight the Buddhas and their Sons. All the supreme accomplishment of these enlightened beings are collected in the form of light which is reabsorbed into the HUM, so that Vajrasattva becomes an accumulation of brightness, power and force.

OM VAJRASATTVA SAMAYA/MANU PALAYA/VAJRASATTVA TENOPA TISHTA/ DRIDHO ME BHAVA/SUTO SHYO ME BHAVA/ SUPO SHYO ME BHAVA/ANURAKTO ME BHAVA/SARVA SIDDHI ME PRAYACCHA/ SARVA KARMA SUCHA ME/CHITTAM SHRIYAM/KURU HUM/HA HA HA HA HO BHAGAWAN/SARVA TATHAGATA/VAJRA MAME MUNCHA/VAJRA BHAVA MAHA SAMAYA SATTVA/A HUM PHAT.

While reciting the mantra distinctly at moderate speed and volume, visualize the nectar from the letters of the mantra filling Vajrasattva's body. They then enter our body through the top of the head, expelling all mental and physical impurities in the form of impure water, scorpions, spiders and other black matter. These leave the body by the lower orifice and enter the earth which cracks and absorbs all the defilements.

Through my ignorance and delusion I have transgressed and damaged my vows,
O Guru, Protector, be my Refuge!
In the Lord, Holder of the Vajra,

Whose essence is the Great Compassion
In the Lord of Beings, I take my Refuge.

Then, Vajrasattva speaks:

O Son of the Family, all your harmful deeds, defilements and transgressions against your vows
are purified and cleansed.

When he has spoken these words, he is absorbed into our-
self and we become endowed with his qualities of body,
speech and mind.

### (8) Dedication of merit

Having thus acquired all these merits and having
done all these skilful actions in the past and
present, empower me to lift the veil of suffering
from all sentient beings. May the merit gained by
my acting thus go to the alleviation of the suffering of all beings. My personalities throughout my
existences, my possessions and my merits, in all
three ways I give up without regard for myself.
Just as the earth and other elements are serviceable in many ways to the infinite number of beings inhabiting limitless space, so may I become
that which maintains all beings so long as all have
not attained peace.

## THE FOUR OPPONENT POWERS

There are four opponent powers which must be applied so
that the purification of non-virtues may be effective.

### a. THE POWER OF REPENTANCE

If one has mistakenly taken poison, one will feel great regret
at having done so. Instead of remembering and enumerat-
ing useless items from our past as we are prone to do, we
should endeavor to remember the unskilful actions per-

formed in this and in previous existences and develop strong and sincere repentance.

b. THE POWER OF THE DECISION NOT TO REPEAT SUCH ACTIONS

If one has eaten something harmful, naturally one will resolve to avoid doing so again. We should make the decision to refrain from such unskilful actions even at the cost of our own lives. If however, we feel too weak to make this ultimate commitment immediately, we should gradually build and reinforce our resolution day by day.

c. THE POWER OF THE OBJECT OF REFUGE

We must take refuge, entrusting ourselves to Vajrasattva as the manifestation of all the Buddhas, and develop bodhichitta. If you trip and fall you use the ground as a support to help you stand up again. All unskilful deeds are committed against the Triple Gem and sentient beings, so to purify the seeds of these actions we must turn for refuge to the Three Jewels and cultivate bodhichitta for the sake of all beings.

d. THE POWER OF REMEDY

Recitation of the mantra of Vajrasattva is the most effective method of counteracting the storage of unskilful karma.

With these four powers we should repeat the hundred syllable mantra at least twenty-one times daily, and continue doing so without omitting a day until we have completed at least one hundred thousand recitations. As we become more deeply involved in this practice, signs of purification will appear recurrently in dreams, such as vomiting impurities, drinking milk or curd, bathing, and so forth. In daily life devotion to the Guru and to the Triple Gem as well as concentration will increase. By reciting this mantra one requests union with Vajrasattva, destroys the seeds of past unskilful karma, and can even purify transgressions against the tantric root vows.

## D. Mandala offering

Mandala means to take the essence. Although this is a simple practice it is an effective means of accumulating merit. It is offered to the Object of Refuge which is free from all impurity and attachment, therefore the practice is for our own benefit.

The mandala base should be a round plate about six inches in diameter; if possible this should be of a precious substance such as silver, but even a stone or wooden surface is adequate. Whatever the material is, it should be visualised as a golden ground, the symbol of the Buddha nature in us. The offering substance can be cleaned grains such as wheat or rice. One can also add precious stones, rings and so forth.

To begin, place a few grains in the left hand and hold the base before yourself at the heart level. With your right hand drop some grain on the center of the base and, while reciting the verses of refuge and generating bodhichitta, wipe off the grain in a clockwise direction three times or more with the right forearm. This signifies the elimination of the three poisons of ignorance, anger and attachment which obscure our Buddha nature. It is done with the right forearm because along it runs the nerve of wisdom.

Now drop some grain on the center of the base and polish three times in an anticlockwise direction. This symbolises our wish to attain the qualities of body, speech and mind of the Buddha.

Then, drop the remaining grain in the hand on to the center of the base and, taking a fresh handful, sprinkle a fence around the edge of the base in a clockwise direction.

Next, form a small heap at the center with one handful of grain, to symbolise Mount Meru; around it are the four continents at each of the cardinal points. Two more heaps on either side of the central one symbolise the sun and the moon.

When this has been done, all the preciousness and beauty of the universe is offered, while reciting the following verses:

> By the virtue of offering to this assemblage of Buddhas visualised before me this mandala, built on a base resplendent with flowers, incense, saffron water, and adorned with Mount Meru, the four continents, the sun and the moon, may all sentient beings share in its good effects.

When the offering has been made, tip the mandala towards yourself and, as the grain falls onto your lap, visualise that you are receiving the blessings of the Object of Refuge.

Although it may seem absurd to attempt to offer the whole universe, by cultivating a mental attitude which predisposes one to offer everything, great results are achieved. Once a king made a great offering to the Buddha and the Sangha. A beggar, seeing this offering, rejoiced at the king's action. The Enlightened One declared that the merit accumulated by that beggar in rejoicing was far greater than that of the king, since the value of no material gift can equal the power of a pure mental offering.

The practice of the Six Perfections is also contained in the mandala offering:

1. To clean the base regularly with a mixture made of saffron and water is the training in the Perfection of Generosity, for water symbolises prosperity and plenty.
2. To look after the base and keep it clean is training in the Perfection of Moral Discipline which is the foundation for this and all practices.
3. To carefully remove insects and worms from the grain before beginning the offering is training in the Perfection of Patience.
4. To offer the mandala with energy and joy is training in the Perfection of Enthusiastic Effort.
5. To offer the mandala with a concentrated mind is training in the Perfection of Meditation.

6.  To offer it with right understanding of the Voidness is training in the Perfection of Wisdom.

There are four levels of mandala offering: outer, inner, secret and absolute. In the preliminary practices described here we are concerned with the outer offering which should be performed one hundred thousand times. The whole meaning of the dharma from the beginning of our practice until the attainment of enlightenment is contained within this practice. Offering the mandala is of great benefit to both the initiated and uninitiated.

## E. *Guru Yoga*

There are many ways of practising Guru Yoga. In the meditation called Guru Puja the visualisation is as depicted on many thangkas. The Guru first appears on a lotus seat at the center of the wish fulfilling tree. From him emanates light which takes the form of countless Buddhas and Bodhisattvas all seated on lotus thrones. This whole assembly is visualised on the wish fulfilling tree and in the space above sits the whole lineage of gurus. However, this is very difficult for the beginner because of its complexity.

Guru Yoga can also be performed in conjunction with one particular meditational deity, for example Maitreya Buddha.

In the space before us we visualise a pure white cloud on which rests a golden throne surmounted by a lotus seat and moon-disc. On this sits Maitreya Buddha in a position which indicates that he is about to rise. His feet rest on a lotus foot-stool; his body is radiant and golden; his hands are in the Dharmacakra mudra at his heart and from them come two flower stems. The flower on his right supports a Dharmacakra, the flower on his left a flask of nectar. His ornaments are rich and brilliant. At the centre of his chest, at his heart, is a small moon-disc on which stands the golden syllable MAI. Around this letter in clockwise direction is the

Guru mantra; surrounding this is the short mantra of Maitreya, and around this is the extended mantra of Maitreya.

If Guru Yoga is performed with Tara as the deity we visualise in the same way a cloud, lotus seat and moon-disc. Seated on this is Tara in the position and with mudra and ornaments as described in the sadhanas. At the heart of this white or green Tara is a white or green TAM; around it stands the Guru mantra, and surrounding this is the Tara mantra both in clockwise direction.

With the Guru Sakyamuni, visualise the seed syllable MUM. If the Guru is visualised as Vajrapani, Vajradhara, or other deities, the procedure is the same, only the outward form, seed syllable, and mantra differ. The most important point to remember is that in whatever form they are visualised, the Guru and the deity are of the same nature. The deity and everything else visualised are all manifestations of the Guru. The purpose of visualising the Guru as a deity is that, since our minds are deluded, to visualise him in his ordinary form might decrease instead of increase our respect, whereas if we see him as an extraordinary being our devotion and reverence will grow. However, we may visualise him in his ordinary form if to see him in such a way does not present us with this difficulty. If the Guru has passed away, we visualise a golden throne with two cushions instead of the lotus seat. When we do this practice with the Guru in his ordinary form we visualise the blue letter HUM at his heart, and around this only the Guru mantra.

Next, we make whatever physical offerings we can and chant the verses of the Seven Limb Puja slowly and as melodiously as possible, while contemplating their meaning. After this, the mandala offering is made seven or twenty-one times. If there is sufficient time the mandala of thirty-seven heaps should be offered seven times. Otherwise the first offering should be the long one and the subsequent offerings should consist of the mandala of seven heaps.Then, with deep respect and faith the Guru mantra is recited, during which we visualise light and nectar emanating from the seed-syllable and from the syllables of the mantras at the Guru's or Deity's heart which shower down upon our head. Within the nectar and light are small radiant letters of the Guru mantra and tiny forms of the Guru or deity which are absorbed into the body at the crown of the head, just as snow becomes one with the water of a lake as soon as it falls on it. As they are absorbed we are cleansed of all impurities. If it is primarily purification we seek, the light and nectar are visualised as white, whereas for physical and spiritual development they are seen as yellow. For the acquisition of power they are seen as red, and as blue if our purpose is to defeat and subdue inner and outer obstacles and evil. After this, we should imagine ourselves as completely pure.

During each meditation on Guru Yoga the Guru mantra should be recited at least one hundred and eight times and the mantra of the deity twenty-one times. The practice is continued until the Guru mantra has been recited one hundred thousand times.

When the recitation of mantras is concluded all the emanations of the Guru return to their source. Then we visualise the Guru on our head becoming smaller until finally he is absorbed into ourselves. At this moment the Guru nature and our own become one. The same procedure is followed if our visualisation of the Guru is in the form of a deity. Between sessions of Guru Yoga during the day, the Guru or deity is not absorbed in this manner, so that when we begin a new period of meditation their form is remembered.

In this practice devotion to our Guru and complete confidence in him are of primary importance. At present there is a great disparity between our Guru's nature and our own; by exerting effort to eliminate the obstacles which separate our nature from his, this disparity will diminish. The attainment of union of our own nature and that of the Guru is the accomplishment of Guru Yoga.

This concludes the explanation of the Extraordinary Preliminary Practices.

## *Conclusion*

In order to practise dharma we should learn about the different traditions and, after finding one which is best suited to ourselves, we should follow it sincerely.

The Buddha came to fulfil the wishes of sentient beings, to end suffering and to attain temporary and permanent happiness. All the various levels of teachings were delivered to individuals of different capacities by the Buddha Sakyamuni, and they are similar in the respect that their aim is one. Therefore, because there is nothing taught by the Buddha that is not beneficial, distinctions such as good and bad, high and low, cannot be made. If any tradition was partially or totally wrong, than it could not have been taught by a Buddha. Moreover, to disparage the teachings is to disparage the Master himself.

The karma produced by such an action is called "abandonment of the dharma", and the Buddha has stated in many sutras that its degree of heaviness cannot be compared with killing as many arhats as there are grains of sand in the Ganges. The practice of dharma is for the abandonment of unskilful actions and for the collection of skilful ones. If simultaneously the teachings are disparaged, it is like taking poison to cure an illness. Knowing this, we should be extremely careful and, whatever tradition we follow, it should be done according to our own capabilities, while respecting equally the other teachings. Complete certainty concerning this can be found in such sutras as the *Saddharma Pundarika Sutra* and the Samadhiraja Sutra.

> May all sentient beings my fathers and mothers
> become endowed with happiness;
> May all the lower realms be constantly empty;
> May the prayers of all the Bodhisattvas be speedily accomplished.

# Notes

1. In the Gelug tradition there are six preliminaries: (i) To clean one's dwelling and arrange the altar; (ii) to make offerings; (iii) to sit in the lotus posture, take refuge and generate Bodhicitta; (iv) to visualise the Object of refuge; (v) to perform the Seven Limb Puja; (vi) to offer the mandala and make the three following requests: (a) to destroy all obstacles, from disrespect to the Guru up to the last obstruction to perfect knowledge of all dharmas; (b) to attain all qualities, from a respectful attitude towards the Guru up to the attainment of perfect buddhahood and (c) to be free from all unfavorable circumstances. Moreover, in special cases people perform more preliminaries such as offering one hundred thousand water bowls, or casting one hundred thousand Buddha images.

2. In the Hinayana tradition one who has committed any of the five heinous crimes cannot attain liberation from samsara in the same lifetime. However, in the Mahayana tradition it is believed that these can be purified through special practices, and even enlightenment can be achieved within that same lifetime.

3. The Tripitaka or the three divisions of the Buddhist canon: the collection of the Vinaya texts or books on moral discipline; the sutras or discourses of the Buddhas; and the Abhidharma or Buddhist metaphysics.

4. The eight worldly concerns for this life are: to be affected by gain and loss, fame and notoriety, praise and blame, happiness and misery.

5. The distracted mind is appeased and remains single-pointed on the object of meditation.

6. The Hinayana tradition says that the parinirvana was the actual death of the Buddha, but for the Mahayana tradition it was the end of that particular manifestation of the Buddha.

7. Arya means 'higher'; higher than ordinary beings who lack the direct cognition of shunyata.

8. Kleshavarana, the obstruction of the afflictions, and jneyavarana, the obstruction of the imprint of the afflictions.